Fictional Justice Based on the True Story
of Baseball's Bizarre 1981 Split Season

THE BIG RED MACHINE'S LAST HURRAH

RANDY & GRANT FREKING

THE BIG RED MACHINE'S LAST HURRAH

Fictional Justice Based on the True Story of Baseball's Bizarre 1981 Split Season

Copyright © Randy Freking / Grant Freking

All rights reserved. No part of this book may be reproduced or transmitted in any form or by any means, electronic or mechanical, including photocopying, recording, or by any information storage or retrieval system, without written permission from the author or the publisher, except for the inclusion of brief quotations in a review.

Published by BookBaby

Greg Eckel, design

Susan Bradley, editor

ISBN: 979-8-35098-753-9

Printed in the United States of America

First Edition, 2024

Photos of Reds players and manager courtesy of Rhodes/Klumpe Reds Hall of Fame Collection.

The use of the Reds logo and the phrase "Big Red Machine" on the front cover is courtesy of a license from Major League Baseball.

Back cover photo courtesy of the Cincinnati Reds.

Dedication

To the Cincinnati Reds, who provided our family
and fellow Reds fans with years of enjoyment, particularly
the members of the Big Red Machine;

To Randy's wife, Sue, who put up with countless hours of
a hermit-like existence while Randy wrote this book
with our nephew, Grant;

To Randy's parents, Bob and Esther Freking,
and Grant's parents, Jay and Debbie Freking,
who inspired our love of baseball;

To the cadre of journalists who inspired
Grant's journalistic enthusiasm; and

To the rest of our families, who have consistently supported us,
even during the COVID-19 pandemic when we
first embarked on this project.

Table of Contents

Dedication		III
Acknowledgements		VII
Introduction		IX
1	**The Wackiest Lawsuit in American Sports History**	1
2	**The Rise, Dominance and Dismantling of the Big Red Machine**	5
3	**Preparing For Battle**	17
4	**Storm Clouds Loom Over the 1981 Season**	23
5	**Help Wanted**	37
6	**A Season Unlike Any Other Begins**	45
7	**The Media Descends on Columbus**	55
8	**A Banner First Half**	65
9	**The Trial Begins**	75
10	**Storm Clouds Lead to Thunder**	81
11	**The Plaintiffs Educate the Judge**	85
12	**Strike Three**	89
13	**Jim Far Becomes a Star**	95
14	**A Long Two Months**	107
15	**Day 2 of the Trial**	119

16	**The Second-Half Folly**	131
17	**Day 3 of the Trial**	139
18	**The Second Half Ends**	151
19	**MLB Defends the Split Season**	161
20	**More Than Just a Big Red Mess**	173
21	**The Decision**	181
22	**Dueling Dynasties**	191
23	**The Reimagined 1981 World Series**	197
24	**Play Ball**	203
25	**The Reds Are in a Familiar Hole**	209
26	**The Machine Gets Into Gear**	215
27	**Bench's Banner Night**	221
28	**Game 5 Reunion**	225
29	**Rain, Rain, Go Away**	233
30	**Reds' History Repeats**	237
31	**Here We Go Again!**	245
	Epilogue - What Really Happened	253
	Fictional World Series Simulation	256
	Bibliography	257
	About the Authors	259

Acknowledgments

This book was a labor of love, and we needed love to complete it over five years of on-again, off-again writing and research.

We thank Randy's law school classmates Jim Neary and Bob Kiss, who provided inspiration for a 1981 lawsuit, and Don Gregory, who often laughed and joked about Randy's unsuccessful venture into court and who meticulously maintained various press materials covering the escapade.

We are particularly grateful to Greg Eckel for his design of the cover and the book's interior. Greg provided valuable insight into the possible names for the book, and his creativity is unmatched. Most of all, we are thankful he has become a friend.

Susan Bradley of North Carolina assisted with early editing of the book. She provided useful comments that we learned from as we continued to write and edit the book. Sue then returned and helped us complete our project. Sue is excellent stylistically and substantively, and easy to work with.

Last, we want to acknowledge the Cincinnati Reds Community Fund for its assistance with photos. A portion of the proceeds from this book will be donated to the Community Fund to support its outstanding work with disadvantaged youth.

Johnny Bench

Dave Concepción

Ken Griffey

George Foster

Introduction

WHAT IF WE TOLD YOU one of baseball's greatest dynasties was deprived of one last World Series run — not by competing teams, but by Major League Baseball team owners? This is the story of the bizarre 1981 MLB season and how the Cincinnati Reds were excluded from the playoffs despite possessing baseball's best record.

It was the last season in which the four remaining members of the world-famous Big Red Machine's "Great Eight" — Johnny Bench, Dave Concepción, George Foster, and Ken Griffey — would play together in Cincinnati. That foursome, complemented by pitching aces Tom Seaver and Mario Soto, and a collection of strong supplemental players, were shut out of the postseason and denied the opportunity to pursue the Reds' third World Series championship in seven years.

We know what you're thinking. How could the best team in baseball not play in October? Well, in June 1981, baseball owners provoked a 50-day strike by the Major League Baseball Players Association after the union and team owners could not reach an agreement on compensation for teams that lost players to free agency. Beginning on June 12, play abruptly stopped for nearly two months, resulting in the cancellation of 713 regular-season games during a season that had the makings of one of the most exciting baseball summers ever. Finally, on July 31, the union and league representatives reached an agreement and prepared to resume the truncated season.

An estimated $146 million was lost in player salaries, ticket sales, broadcast revenues, and concession revenues. The players forfeited over $28 million in salaries, while the 26 owners suffered a net loss of $28 million (after strike insurance alleviated some of the pain). The union won the battle, though, as the essential elements of free agency remained in place.

After the strike was over, MLB and Commissioner Bowie Kuhn devised a playoff structure that team owners hoped would keep the majority of teams in postseason contention, attempting to maximize engagement from fans disgusted by the work stoppage. And more importantly, team owners desired a mechanism to recover at least some of the lost revenue. Kuhn announced that in both the National League and the American League, the team with the best record in its respective division (East or West) prior to the strike would be awarded an automatic berth in the postseason. Its first-round opponent would be the team in its division with the best record for the second half of the season. The winners of those four matchups would face off to determine the league champions and then, as in a normal year, the two league champions would move on to contend in the World Series. This "split-season" approach had not been used in professional baseball for 90 years.

In 1892, the National League announced before the season that it would split its season in an attempt to increase fan interest following the collapse of the rival

> American Association. The Boston Beaneaters won the first half of the season, and the Cleveland Spiders took the second half. In the championship series, Boston defeated Cleveland five games to none, with one tie. Not even Bowie Kuhn had the gumption to rely on that aberration as any sort of precedent.

As critics of this unusual playoff modification were quick to point out, this approach completely eroded the importance of a team's season-long win-loss record. All that mattered were team standings at the point when the strike commenced and when the season ended.

The cockamamie split-season structure left two deserving teams, the Cincinnati Reds and the St. Louis Cardinals, out of the playoffs. Again, the Reds compiled the best cumulative record in all of baseball that year. The Cardinals had the best overall record in the NL East. Under Kuhn's scheme, MLB awarded playoff spots to teams that would never have qualified for the postseason under normal rules. For a sport that prides itself on maintaining traditions, this was venturing into the theater of the absurd, as preposterous as Barry Larkin in a Dodger uniform or the proprietors of Skyline giving away their sacred chili recipe.

Kuhn considered himself a baseball purist, but this decision was purely about attendance, television ratings, and the almighty dollar. Millions of baseball diehards, already irritated by having missed 50 days of the summer game, strongly opposed a playoff format whose sole purpose was to line owners' pockets and maximize MLB's revenue. It didn't seem to matter that teams with the best overall records were being excluded from the playoffs just because they didn't finish in first place at two designated points in time.

In response to what fans viewed as an affront to baseball's integrity, three Ohio State University law students filed suit in United States District Court in Columbus, Ohio, to prevent the playoffs from proceeding. On October 5, 1981, they sought an injunction to halt the first round of playoff games and to insert the teams with the best overall divisional records into the playoffs.

In the odd-numbered chapters from 1 through 21, we play fast and loose with the facts and provide a fictional rendition of what might have happened had the law students' case gone to court. The imaginary court case describes fictional lawyers, courtroom characters, proceedings, dialogue, and testimony that the students dreamed would happen. The dialogue attributed to baseball figures during the trial, including Commissioner Bowie Kuhn, is fantasy based on factual research. The resulting World Series (beginning with Chapter 23) is entirely fictional as well, though it could have occurred but for the travesty manufactured by Kuhn. We hope you will have as much fun reading it as we had writing it.

Chapter 2 recounts the origin, ascent, and steady disassembling of the Big Red Machine. We also analyze the underlying labor dispute behind the players' strike that needlessly interrupted play. In even-numbered chapters from Chapters 4 through 22, we provide the *true account* of the origins of the labor dispute, the strange and unprecedented 1981 season, and the mid-season work stoppage. All fiction aside, it is an uncontested fact that the Big Red Machine was one of the greatest dynasties to grace a baseball diamond. As such, we provide extensive background on the Reds during that period precisely because the 1981 season marked the last hurrah for perhaps the best collection of baseball talent ever. This final act for the Machine contributed to an enormously exciting 1981 season— up until the strike, of course—for the Reds and for baseball as a whole. Cincinnati's regular season win percentage topped baseball in 1981 and remains among the best in the history of baseball's oldest franchise. It's time this special group earned some long overdue respect.

Our fictional account begins with the filing of the lawsuit intended to stop the playoffs from proceeding. To advance their noble cause, the three law students must convince a judge to right baseball's wrongs—and to do so quickly, given the need to conduct the "Fall Classic" before bad weather rolls in. A just decision could result in the most-watched World Series of all-time.

"Baseball is something more than a game to an American boy; it is his training field for life work. Destroy his faith in its squareness and honesty and you have destroyed something more; you have planted suspicion of all things in his heart."

JUDGE KENESAW MOUNTAIN LANDIS
FIRST COMMISSIONER OF BASEBALL

1

The Wackiest Lawsuit in American Sports History

OCTOBER 1, 1981

THE CINCINNATI REDS and the St. Louis Cardinals were both in second place in their respective National League divisions. That put them within striking distance of the second-half championship, but with only three games left in the regular season, time was running out to capture first place. According to the highly irregular playoff format cobbled together by Commissioner Bowie Kuhn, second place was not going to be good enough to move on to the postseason, even though the Reds and the Cardinals sported superior season-long records compared to their division rivals.

Three Ohio State University law students—Bob Smack, Jim Far, and Randy Queen—were not going to take this injustice sitting down. According to baseball's hallowed traditions, the best team in each league earned the right to compete in the postseason. Smack, Far, and Queen knew time was of the essence. With the playoffs scheduled to begin the following Tuesday, something had to be done!

If the Reds and Cardinals did not win the second half and were denied playoff appearances, Smack, Far, and Queen intended to urge a federal judge to issue a temporary restraining order to halt the playoffs. They wanted the court to insert the Reds and Cardinals into the postseason and disqualify four other teams from the controversial eight-team playoffs.

Smack, Far, and Queen were hardly casual baseball fans. Despite attending law school in Columbus—a solid 110 miles away from Riverfront Stadium in Cincinnati—the three young men had attended many of the Reds' 53 home games during the abbreviated season, still managing to achieve solid Bs and Cs in their classes. The trio were roommates and were daily listeners to Reds, Tigers, and Cardinals games if they were not at Riverfront Stadium.

The students were die-hard baseball fans and thought this might be the last opportunity to see the four remaining members of Cincinnati's Big Red Machine win a World Series. They also knew that thousands of Reds fans purchased season ticket packages, which meant the Reds ticket office guaranteed their eligibility to buy tickets for those same seats for postseason games.

And so, on Friday, October 2, at 7:30 a.m., Queen's Chevy Monza pulled out of an apartment complex on Columbus's west side. The three accomplices were bleary-eyed. Along with their friend, Suzy, they had spent the entire night typing a final version of their class action complaint and an accompanying motion for a temporary restraining order. The papers were footnoted with comments about what could happen over the last weekend of the season to make their concerns moot—particularly if the Reds and Cardinals swept their season-ending series.

They rushed to a copy shop on High Street. There, they made a copy of their court pleadings so they could fax a copy to each MLB team, MLB headquarters, and newspapers around the country. After hovering over a copy machine for three hours, inserting dimes and quarters, they darted to the federal courthouse on Marconi Boulevard in downtown Columbus.

They got lost, but a gas station worker pointed them in the right direction. They assumed their destination was the clerk's office in the courthouse.

Once inside the clerk's office, the students presented their complaint to a bewildered gentleman, Chick Gandil. "You are filing a lawsuit against Major League Baseball?" he asked.

Queen replied without hesitation, "Yes, sir, this is all about corrective justice." (Queen had heard the phrase "corrective justice" while discussing the potential case with friend Dean Frontscheider at Mehlman's Pub, a local bar, the previous week, and he liked the ring of it.) "And we want a hearing on our motion for a temporary restraining order as soon as possible before Tuesday." The students had learned in their trial practice seminar that Rule 65 of the Federal Rules of Civil Procedure allowed for almost immediate attention to a request for an injunction, and a temporary restraining order, or TRO, was the first step.

Gandil, it turned out, was a longtime baseball fan. "Well, you're correct—the Reds and Cardinals are getting hosed. But do you kids really think you can stop the playoffs?"

"If the court is here to do justice, why not?" asked Far. "How soon can we see a judge?"

Gandil explained the process. The chief judge would receive the papers and decide whether to assign it to another judge or keep it himself. The Honorable Joseph Jackson was chief judge, and Gandil guessed he would keep the case because "he will find this very interesting." Added Gandil, "One of you will probably get a call before 5:00 p.m., and the court will let you know if a hearing is scheduled."

Queen, Smack, and Far returned to the copy shop and spent the next couple of hours faxing copies seemingly everywhere. Then they scurried to their car, drove to Mehlman's, and spent the rest of the day telling anyone who would listen why their TRO was necessary.

A once-in-a-lifetime collection of talent recovers from early postseason stumbles to cement its reputation in baseball lore.

2
The Rise, Dominance and Dismantling of the Big Red Machine

IN THE 1960S, and before MLB diluted the World Series by expanding the postseason field in 1969, the Cincinnati Reds were beginning their march toward becoming one of the game's best teams. Pete Rose (debuted in 1963), Tony Perez (1964), and Johnny Bench (1967) were the first three cogs in the Big Red Machine. The origin of the "Big Red Machine" moniker is disputed. Some claim it was first used by Bob Hunter of the *Los Angeles Examiner*; others credit Bob Hertzel of *The Cincinnati Enquirer*. When Hertzel used the phrase "The Big Red Machine" in a July 1969 article, it was in reference to the Reds' powerful offense that paced the National League in runs (by 73), home runs (by 29), and total bases (by 141). However, the team finished third in the NL's West division that year.

The fledgling dynasty took off in 1970, winning 70 of its first 100 games—yes, that's right—en route to a 102-60 record, the best in the National League. Following a three-game sweep of the Pittsburgh Pirates in the National League Championship Series (NLCS), Cincinnati was on the precipice of its first World Series championship since 1940. But the 108-win Baltimore Orioles, making their third World Series appearance in five years, took care of the confident Reds in five games, limiting first-year manager Sparky Anderson's club to a .213 batting average. A pair of Hall of Fame-bound Robinsons—Frank (a former Red) and the World Series MVP, Brooks—carried Baltimore and delivered a hearty helping of humble pie.

The Reds endured a down year in 1971, going 79-83, but they bounced back in 1972. Buoyed by an offseason trade with the Houston Astros for All-Star second baseman Joe Morgan, outfielder Cesar Geronimo, and starting pitcher Jack Billingham, the Reds ran away with the NL West, clearing the second-place Los Angeles Dodgers by 10.5 games. Bench clobbered 40 home runs en route to his second MVP award. Perez (first base) and Rose (left field) had changed positions, while Dave Concepción was establishing himself as the team's primary shortstop. Cincinnati's offense remained potent, ranking second in the NL in runs scored, while also strengthening its defense through strong pitching. The Reds' pitching staff ranked third in the league in earned run average (ERA). Starting pitchers Billingham, Ross Grimsley, and Gary Nolan won between 12 and 15 games, and none of the three had an ERA above 3.18. In the bullpen, Clay Carroll tallied 37 saves, and Tom Hall and Pedro Borbon posted ERAs of 2.61 and 3.17, respectively.

In 1972, the path to the World Series was far bumpier—but also much more thrilling—than it had been in 1970. The Reds fell behind the Pirates two games to one in their best-of-five NLCS matchup. In Game 4, Grimsley pitched a complete-game two-hitter in a 7-1 Cincinnati victory. In Game 5 at Riverfront Stadium, the hosts trailed 3-2 entering the bottom of the ninth inning. It was in this inning that the Machine began to flash its propensity for clutch postseason moments. Bench led off with an opposite-field home run to tie the game. Reds radio play-by-play broadcaster Al Michaels' call of the round-tripper barely registered among the hysterics of the home crowd. Perez then followed with a single. Denis Menke singled George Foster (pinch running for Perez) to second. After Geronimo flew out and moved Foster to third, Darrel Chaney popped out in the infield. Hal McRae stood in versus Bob Moose with a chance to send Cincinnati to the World Series. As it turns out, McRae only needed to stand in the box, as Moose spiked a breaking ball nowhere near the plate, allowing Foster to score the series-clinching run on the wild pitch.

In the World Series, the Reds were pitted against the Oakland Athletics, owners of the AL's best regular-season record. Oakland, the visiting team, prevailed in a pair of one-run games in Games 1 and 2, with future Hall of Famers Rollie Fingers and Catfish Hunter, as well as former MVP Vida Blue and All-Star Ken Holtzman, keeping the Reds' powerful offense at bay by letting in only three runs. Billingham pitched an eight-inning masterpiece in Game 3, allowing no runs and just three hits, with seven strikeouts. In Game 4, the Reds were clinging to a 2-1 lead in the ninth inning, but Borbon and Carroll could not hold the fort. The A's tallied four straight one-out singles to prevail, positioning themselves within a single victory of the franchise's first title since 1930. However, the Reds finally reversed the tide versus Hunter and Fingers in Game 5, escaping with a 5-4 decision via run-scoring hits in the eighth inning by Bobby Tolan and in the ninth inning by Rose, who had also led off the game with a home run. Game 6 was the lone tilt in the series not decided by a single run; the Reds rocked Blue and the rest of the A's pitching for 10 hits in an 8-1 rout.

Riverfront Stadium hosted Game 7 on October 22 before a crowd of 56,040. Oakland inched ahead in the top of the first, with Gene Tenace plating Angel Mangual after Mangual reached on a three-base error by Tolan in center field. The pitchers' duel between Hunter and Billingham produced further zeros by each squad until McRae, pinch-hitting for Billingham, drove in Perez with a bases-loaded sacrifice fly in the bottom of the fifth. Rose flew out to deep right-center to end the threat. The A's responded immediately versus Borbon in the sixth. Following Bert Campaneris's leadoff single, Mangual advanced Campaneris to second with a bunt, and Joe Rudi moved Campaneris to third with a groundout to Morgan at second base. But Tenace came through once more, sending a double to deep left field, regaining the lead for Oakland. The next batter, Sal Bando, doubled in Allan Lewis, who had pinch run for Tenace. The visitors were up 3-1, just 12 outs away from glory.

The Reds would not exit quietly, however. While facing Hunter on the mound, Cincinnati had runners on second and third with two outs in the sixth, but Menke flew out. In the home half of the eighth, the Reds scratched across a run against Fingers on a sacrifice fly by Perez. Once again, runners were on second and third base for Menke. And once again, he flew out. (In Menke's defense, he was battling future Hall of Famers in tense moments.) With two outs in the ninth, Chaney advanced to first when Fingers hit him on the shin, but Rose flew out to left-center, and Oakland secured its championship. Tenace, who hit .348 with nine RBI in 23 at-bats during the Series, was named MVP, a surprising ascent after registering a measly .225 batting average in 227 regular-season at-bats.

The Reds won 99 games in 1973 and 98 games in 1974, but they failed to reach the World Series in either year, or even the postseason in 1974. In 1973, Cincinnati dropped the deciding Game 5 of the NLCS to the New York Mets, with Tom Seaver the winning pitcher, and in 1974, the Reds finished four games behind the 102-win Los Angeles Dodgers.

Cincinnati returned to the postseason with a vengeance in 1975 and 1976, cementing the Big Red Machine's undeniable place in the upper echelon of MLB history. In 1975, the 108-win Reds swept the Pirates 3-0 in the NLCS before their memorable encounter with the Boston Red Sox in the World Series, a seven-game clash regarded as one of the best Fall

Classics ever and one in which Cincinnati was actually outscored 30-29.

In the 1975 matchup, the clubs split the first four games, with Games 2, 3, and 4 all decided by one run. In Game 5 at Riverfront Stadium, Cincinnati won 6-2 behind Perez's decisive three-run homer in the sixth inning. Because of a travel day and continuous rain in Boston, four full days passed between Games 5 and 6. When Game 6 finally happened on October 21, the Reds fell behind 3-0 after the first inning. Griffey's two-run triple and Bench's run-scoring single in the fifth leveled the score. Foster doubled in Griffey and Morgan in the seventh, and Geronimo smacked a solo home run in the eighth. But Bernie Carbo, a former Red, crushed a three-run bomb off Rawly Eastwick to deep center field to tie the score in the home half of the eighth. This unforgettable game made its way into extra innings, with Carlton Fisk's drive off Fenway Park's left-field foul pole ending the affair in the 12th inning during the early hours of Sunday morning on the East Coast.

The next day (or hours later, in actuality), the Big Red Machine spent most of Game 7 behind, surrendering three runs in the third inning. In the sixth, Perez walloped Bill Lee's eephus pitch over the left-field Green Monster and deep into the Boston night to bring the visitors within one. The Reds tied the game in the seventh when Griffey walked, stole second, and scored on Rose's two-out single to center. In the top of the ninth, Griffey led off with a walk. He moved to second on Geronimo's sacrifice bunt and to third on a groundout by Dan Driessen. After Rose, the eventual World Series MVP, worked a full-count walk off reliever Jim Burton, Morgan, the NL MVP in 1975, blooped a two-out, go-ahead single to short center field. Will McEnaney pitched a 1-2-3 ninth for the Reds' first World Series crown in 35 years. After years of falling just short of a championship, the Big Red Machine had finally reached the pinnacle of the sport, winning one of the most thrilling World Series in baseball history. And with the team's essential components returning for a repeat run in 1976, the Reds weren't about to let another chance at prestige slip by. Rather, they would unleash the full might of the Machine.

As regular season wins go, the 1976 Reds, with 102 wins, weren't quite as successful as the 1975 squad, but the difference between the two iterations was the unrelenting postseason dominance by the reigning champs. After clearing the second-place Dodgers by 10 games in the NL West, Cincinnati swept Philadelphia in three games in the NLCS, outscoring the Phillies 19-11. The Reds took the first two contests with relative ease, but Game 3 was a classic. Trailing visiting Philadelphia 3-0 in the bottom of the seventh, the Big Red Machine roared into high gear. After Griffey singled, Morgan walked, and Perez singled, Foster's sacrifice fly brought Cincinnati within one. A walk by Bench and an out later, Geronimo tripled in both Perez and Bench to push the hosts ahead 4-3. However, the Phillies recovered and led 6-4 entering the bottom of the ninth.

No lead was safe versus the Machine, though. Foster and Bench led off the ninth with back-to-back solo home runs to level the score. Bench's dinger was nearly four years to the day from his game-tying home run in the ninth inning versus Pittsburgh in Game 5 of the 1972 NLCS. Upon his return to the dugout, Bench was mobbed by his teammates, greeted first by Morgan, Perez, and Rose. After a pitching change, Concepción singled and Geronimo walked. Ed Armbrister, pinch-hitting for Eastwick, sacrificed the runners to second and third. Rose was handed an intentional free pass, bringing Griffey to the plate. The outfielder bashed the ball into the Riverfront turf, leaving plenty of time for Concepción to scoot home and secure the Reds' fourth NL pennant in six years.

The New York Yankees awaited in the World Series, owners of an American League–best 97 victories during the regular season and boasting the AL's top pitching staff in terms of ERA. The rotation was headed by

Hunter, who had signed as a free agent prior to the 1975 season. The Bronx Bombers—with AL MVP Thurman Munson on the roster—turned out to be no match for the Reds, yielding 22 runs on 42 hits in the four-game sweep. Bench, the World Series MVP, notched eight hits in 15 at-bats, half of which were extra-base knocks. In Game 4, Bench smacked a pair of home runs. The hitting barrage mirrored the Reds' regular season output; the club led the NL in runs, batting average, doubles, triples, home runs, RBI, stolen bases, on-base percentage and slugging percentage. On the rubber, eight Cincinnati pitchers combined for a 2.00 ERA and limited the Yankees, the AL's second-best offense, to eight runs. The Big Red Machine had officially become baseball's latest dynasty. No National League team since has captured consecutive world championships. And given that the 1976 opponent was the Yankees, the victory was particularly sweet.

Said Billingham, "We didn't hate them, but they were always the team, the most popular team. Everywhere you go across the country, you'd see New York hats. We played them four games, won and went home. We swept them, which was wonderful. It was exciting to sweep."

And while the winning continued as the 1970s came to a close, no more World Series titles would follow for more than a decade. Fearing an inflated payroll in years to come, general manager Bob Howsam traded Perez, then 34, to the Montreal Expos in December 1976, less than two months after the Reds' thorough domination of the Yankees and even the rest of baseball. Howsam was regarded as the chief architect of the Big Red Machine, which had been built through shrewd trades and the Reds' renowned farm system—all prior to the advent of free agency. Howsam and Dick Wagner, Howsam's top lieutenant and ultimate successor, believed small-market teams could not compete with large-market teams for talent after the advent of free agency in December 1975. (Howsam would later acknowledge that the Perez trade was his biggest mistake.)

Manager Sparky Anderson, the Machine's crankshaft, regarded Perez as the heart and soul of the team, and he worried that Perez could not be effectively replaced. Howsam and Wagner then engaged in a bitter contract dispute with Rose that was not resolved until the eve of Opening Day in 1977. Describing Rose's disagreement with the Reds as bitter might actually be underselling the situation; Rose was quoted by *The Washington Post* as threatening to fine the Reds $25,000 a month until the All-Star break if his demands for $400,000 a season were not met. "If a player doesn't sign and doesn't join the club, he is fined a thousand bucks a day," Rose said. "I'm just doing the same thing [to them]."

The Reds countered Rose's demands by taking out full-page, 1,500-word ads in a pair of local newspapers to lay out their arguments against Rose. Wagner's bold public relations tactic against the beloved Cincinnati native was incredibly witless, but the audacity of such a maneuver was almost to be admired. *Almost.* Ultimately, Howsam blinked. Rose signed a two-year contract at $375,000 per year. Hertzel announced the good news to fans on the morning of the season opener: "Nighttime is still dark. Stars still twinkle in the sky. Spring still means love. And Pete Rose is still a Cincinnati Red. Opening Day and all's right with the world."

Howsam predicted that there would never again be a team comparable to the Big Red Machine because of the star players' newfound right of free agency, and Wagner agreed. Wagner thought Rose's contract was too expensive, but Rose was a hometown legend. The Rose negotiations left Howsam and Wagner thinking their nightmare was coming true.

The 1977 Reds won 88 games, their lowest win total in six years, and they placed second in the NL West, 10 games behind the Dodgers. This was in spite of the June acquisition of future Hall of Fame starting pitcher Tom Seaver. Foster, on the strength of 52 home runs and 149 RBI, both of which remain club records, won the NL MVP. That made it six NL MVP awards in seven years for Cincinnati—Bench in 1970 and 1972, Rose in 1973, and Morgan in 1975 and 1976.

Howsam gave up his general manager position to Wagner after the 1977 season.

The Reds finished second in the NL West again in 1978, improving their record to 92-69, but they placed 2.5 games short of the Dodgers, who went on to lose to the Yankees in the World Series for the second straight year. With the exception of Perez, every member of the Great Eight remained on the team and was productive at the plate. Cincinnati finished second in the NL in runs and posted its usual strong offensive numbers. Pitching was a different story, though. Even with Seaver helming the rotation, the Reds' pitching staff finished ninth in the NL in ERA. The highlight of the season was Rose's 44-game hitting streak, 12 short of the record set by Joe DiMaggio, which was chronicled by the national press as he chased the "unbreakable" record. Rose's streak is still the longest in National League history.

The lead-up to the 1979 season was fraught with change. Wagner quickly drew the ire of Reds fans when, in his second year succeeding Howsam, he did the unthinkable—he fired Sparky Anderson. Wagner lowered the boom in late November 1978 after the Reds' skipper reportedly refused to replace members of his coaching staff. According to Anderson, Wagner waited to fire him to prevent the manager from signing with another club for the 1979 season. Anderson was replaced by John McNamara, who lasted as manager through the 1982 season. Wagner then failed to sign Rose, who by then was viewed by Wagner as a loathsome free agent. The fans felt otherwise. In early December 1978, Rose signed a four-year deal with Philadelphia, a team he would lead to its first-ever world championship in 1980.

Despite the turnover and a worse record in 1979 (90-71) than the team had achieved in 1978, six members of the Big Red Machine remained. The club won the NL West by a game and a half over the Houston Astros. Cincinnati's return to the postseason was brief, though, as the 98-win Pirates, the eventual World Series champs, swept the Reds in three games. Cincinnati lost the first two games in extra innings (11 innings in Game 1, 10 innings in Game 2) before a 7-1 humbling in Game 3.

The decade ended with the "Team of the '70s" reaching four World Series, winning two. The Reds won six NL West crowns in the decade, winning at least 100 games once and at least 90 games eight times. Cincinnati's worst regular-season record was its 79-83 mark in 1971. In 1975–76, the Reds became the first National League outfit to repeat as World Series champions since the 1921–22 New York Giants. The Big Red Machine's star power spoke for itself. Bench, who went on to be inducted in the National Baseball Hall of Fame in 1989, was regarded as the greatest catcher of his era (and maybe all-time). Bench was joined in Cooperstown by Morgan (1990) and Perez (2000). Rose eventually became the all-time "Hit King." Foster, Griffey, Concepción, and Geronimo, the less-heralded members of the Great Eight, combined for 17 All-Star appearances over the course of their careers. So what would the 1980s bring for the aging, slowly-being-depleted Big Red Machine?

Wagner continued to fear free agency and allowed Morgan to leave after the 1979 season. The 1980 Reds won 89 games and finished third in the NL West. Wagner then traded Geronimo, a three-time Gold Glove–winning center fielder, to Kansas City before the 1981 season. The only remaining members of the Machine for the 1981 season were Bench, Concepción, Foster, and Griffey.

Because of the birth of free agency, Wagner said, "Baseball will never be the same." Ironically, he was correct, though not in the way he imagined. Baseball prospered after free agency with higher attendance, larger TV contracts, and competitive seasons involving both small- and large-market teams. (In fairness to Wagner, Kuhn nixed his attempted trade for Vida Blue, a former Cy Young–winning starter, in January 1978.) Naturally, Wagner wasn't against improving the Reds; he just wasn't going to do so using the free agent market created in 1975. This decision shortened the dynasty's lifespan.

Reds fans who had followed the team throughout the 1970s were spoiled. They were accustomed to success. With four members of the Machine still on the roster, hopes were high for a World Series appearance in 1981. But when MLB concocted a scheme that would dash those hopes, someone needed to intervene.

"Every time we look at the split season standings, the nonsense of a mini playoff, the decimated statistics of an asterisk season, we [will be] reminded of baseball's ugliest episode."

THOMAS BOSWELL
THE WASHINGTON POST

3
Preparing For Battle

FAR, SMACK, AND QUEEN KNEW ONE THING: their lawsuit would have the support of most sports fans. Baseball fans believed the MLB playoff scheme was illegitimate and thought the Reds and their fans in particular were potential victims. As it became evident during the last week of the season's second half that the Cardinals and Reds could be cheated, the three would-be lawyers became increasingly apoplectic and plotted their potential legal challenge. Far was a baseball purist and a Tigers fan, and he cried foul even though his favorite team was not shortchanged.

From Monday through Thursday, the three skipped their law school classes and instead began assembling evidence. The Reds and Cardinals were still in the hunt for the playoffs, but they needed help from other teams to overcome the Houston Astros and the Montreal Expos in the second half. The three fans lamented, "We need to be ready to deal with this travesty."

Law school had taught the three friends how to research extensively, and The Ohio State University Moritz Law Library was among the best in the country. In addition to legal books, the library had scores of newspapers, periodicals, and books in hard copy and on microfiche. The three students divided up the work. Smack was charged with finding evidence to support the idea that season ticket holders relied on promises by clubs that they would be rewarded with the opportunity to purchase postseason tickets if their team had the best record at the end of the season. This information would serve as the linchpin of their legal argument of promissory estoppel, a little-used alternative to a breach of contract claim or an actual contract claim.

Smack was also charged with writing the lawsuit papers, known as "pleadings." As an undergrad, Queen had been a journalism student at the University of Dayton, so he was tasked with combing newspapers from around the country to demonstrate widespread outrage. The friends knew that evidence of anger from fans and sports columnists would make it easier to promote their legal claim, and Far wanted to stir national interest in protests. He called every baseball beat writer in the country to leak their plan and to encourage picketing of MLB's headquarters. The strategy found some success, as *The New York Times* ran a small article about the possibility of a class action lawsuit, and groups of fans began to picket on Wednesday, September 30, in front of MLB headquarters.

For his part, Far was a wannabe baseball historian. He jumped on the tasks of compiling the history of the World Series since 1903, preparing a summary of each team's season-long performance in 1981, and chronicling baseball's labor relations history.

On Thursday, October 1, the law students met to organize their research findings in preparation for their court presentation. The result was 24 bankers boxes of papers in discrete files.

- "World Series Participant Records" were housed in box 1.
- "Season Ticket Solicitations" filled box 2, including letters from various clubs promoting postseason tickets as a bonus for season-ticket purchasers.
- "Pre-1969" was the label on box 3. The contents included research on how postseason baseball was conducted before each league was split into two divisions.
- Box 4 was called "1969–1980 Joke," a pointed reference to the diluted playoff structure in place since the advent of the East and West regions.
- Box 5, called "Press Clippings," included largely negative articles from newspapers and magazines around the country about the split-season concept adopted by MLB in 1981.
- Boxes 6 to 13 contained files on each MLB team broken down by "First Half" and "Second Half" results.
- Research on the primary figures involved in negotiations and the labor concerns at issue were in boxes 14 through 16.
- "Legal Research and Pleadings" made up boxes 17 through 19.
- "Black Sox Scandal" filled boxes 20 through 24.

While Far, Smack, and Queen were hard at work, the grassroots movement had grown to include hundreds of fans picketing MLB headquarters, with placards reading "WE DEMAND A REAL WORLD SERIES." Various protesters were heard to yell, "OWNERS SOLD US OUT" and "IMPEACH KUHN."

Sportswriter Thomas Boswell of *The Washington Post* echoed the fans' unhappiness: "Every time we look at the split-season standings, the nonsense of a mini playoff, the decimated statistics of an asterisk season, we [will be] reminded of baseball's ugliest episode."

To Queen, a student of labor law, the tension between fans and league officials did not come as a surprise. He had sensed that an ugly 1981 labor battle was inevitable ever since the conclusion of the 1980 season.

mbus Citizen-Journal   ★★★   Tues., Oct. 6, 1981

hree fans sue to end playoffs

By STEVE LUTTNER

Three disgruntled Columbus baseball fans are trying to get a federal court judge to stop the major league playoff games.

The three men, all of whom are 24-year-old, third-year law students at Ohio State University, filed suit Monday in U.S. District Court against baseball Commissioner Bowie Kuhn and five playoff-bound teams.

The suit protests this year's unique playoff schedule, which was devised after the baseball players' strike ended. The suit also is seeking $150,000 in damages.

"The money is not a major issue in the suit," said James G. Neary, who added that he and two friends, Robert S. Kiss and Randy Freking, did not file the suit as a publicity stunt.

"What we're trying to do is get an injunction to have the playoffs enjoined. We're trying to downplay our law school affiliation as much as possible. We're just three baseball fans who are just kind of upset with the whole setup."

The playoffs are scheduled to begin Tuesday. Although a hearing had not been scheduled, Neary said he hopes to [...] Tuesday morn[ing...] representing [...] four [...]

BASEBALL SUIT STUDIED — Three Ohio State University students who sued major league baseball Monday study a copy of the lawsuit they filed in U.S. District Court. They are (from left) Robert Kiss, Randy Freking and James Neary. They filed the suit because they believe this year's playoff schedule is unfair. (C-J Photo by A[...] Pennell)

The Cincinnati Reds and the St. Louis Cardinals, for example, posted the best overall winning percentages for the entire year in their respective divisions, but because they did not finish first during either half of the season, they are not in the playoffs.

For that reason, the suit names five of the eight division winners as defendants, because those five teams did not post the best overall record. The teams named in the suit are the Houston Astros, the Los Angeles Dodgers, the Kansas City Royals, the New York Yankees and the Philadelphia Phillies.

Two of the eight teams in the playoffs, the Milwaukee Brewers and the Oakland A's, had the best overall records in their divisions and aren't named in the suit.

The eighth playoff team, the Montreal Expos, are not named in the suit because U.S. District Court does not have jurisdiction in Canada.

Neary, who said he is a Detroit Ti-

gers fan, said he, Freking attended a number of baseb[all...] this year. Freking is a Reds' Kiss' favorite team is the [...] Neary said.

"Plaintiffs have been [...] league baseball for 20 y[ears...] relied on the past prac[tice...] league baseball teams [...] teams with the best r[ecords...] entire season be perm[itted...] post-season play," the [suit...]

"Plaintiffs have n[...] decisions of defenda[nt...] Bowie Kuhn which [...] the integrity of base[ball...] ficed by the whim [...] ented owners whe[...] for their legions [of fans...] tinues.

They three [...] suffered, are su[...] ue to suffer [...] psychological [...] loss of faith [in major...] league baseb[all...]

Ego and greed engender the perfect opportunity for a disaster.

4

Storm Clouds Loom Over the 1981 Season

IN THE MONTHS FOLLOWING THE 1980 SEASON, six years of a contentious relationship between baseball's billionaires, millionaires, and wannabe millionaires came to a head.

Acrimony between MLB team owners and the Major League Baseball Players Association (MLBPA) and its members over the issue of free agent compensation was intense after the "Seitz decisions" of 1974 and 1975. Arbitrator Peter Seitz issued rulings that abolished the "reserve clause" that had been part of baseball since 1880. The clause, which had been in every player's contract, prohibited players who signed with one team to leave for another team unless the owner gave the player an "unconditional release."

The first Seitz decision resulted from one team's failure to honor a player contract. On February 11, 1974, Catfish Hunter agreed with the Oakland A's on a two-year, $200,000 contract with a clause stipulating that $50,000 payments be made to a life insurance annuity of his choosing in each of the next two seasons. After A's owner Charlie Finley refused to make payment on the annuity once he discovered he had to pay $25,000 in taxes—due immediately—the breach of contract dispute headed to an arbitration hearing. On December 13, Seitz, an arbitrator selected by the owners, ruled in favor of Hunter. Finley had breached the contract, and Seitz declared Hunter a "free agent" with the ability to negotiate with any club.

"We don't belong to anybody," Hunter reportedly told his wife.

Six days later, after Commissioner Kuhn gave up on his directive that no owner could bid for Hunter while Finley weighed his appeal options, the Catfish sweepstakes began. Hunter became the highest-paid player in baseball and the highest-paid pitcher in history when he signed a five-year contract with the New York Yankees worth $3.35 million.

Marvin Miller was the MLBPA's hard-nosed executive director. Miller and the players watched Hunter exercise his newfound freedom to play wherever he wanted. He was courted by 23 of the 24 MLB teams, including the A's. Hunter ultimately refused higher offers from the San Diego Padres and the Kansas City Royals in order to ink a contract with the Yankees. Hunter helped the Yankees return to the World Series in 1976 against the Big Red Machine, ending a 12-year absence from postseason baseball for what is arguably America's most famous sports franchise. Yankees owner George Steinbrenner went on to sign six-time All-Star Reggie Jackson prior to the 1977 season, and the Yankees returned to the Series in 1977 and 1978, winning in both years.

MLB owners viewed the 1974 Seitz I decision as narrow; in their view, Hunter became a free agent only because of Finley's gaffe. But Miller saw an opening and filed a grievance in October 1975 seeking free agency for two more pitchers and the abolishment of the reserve clause.

Los Angeles star pitcher Andy Messersmith was at loggerheads with the Dodgers' front office over his 1975 contract, and he played that season without a contract. Another pitcher, Dave McNally, sat out the 1975 campaign with an injury, having had no contract since 1974. In early October 1975, just after the regular season concluded, Miller filed a grievance asking that the two be declared free agents on the grounds that the reserve clause was illegal.

Meanwhile as the Big Red Machine and the Boston Red Sox played in one of the greatest World Series ever, the lords of baseball were on edge: Would Seitz declare the reserve clause illegal? Should we relieve Seitz of his duties and appoint someone else? Though the reserve clause seemed antiquated, a majority of teams believed Seitz would deny free agency to players who had no contract breach such as the one committed by Finley. Their backup plan was a public relations strategy that would sell baseball fans and players on the idea that free agency would wreck baseball. Ultimately, they decided to take their chances with Seitz even though he had surprised them just a year earlier.

After the Messersmith and McNally arbitration hearing, Seitz sat down with Miller and John Gaherin, the team owners' negotiator. Seitz told them he had made a decision, but he encouraged the two parties to negotiate the issue of free agency rather than have him render a decision. Miller agreed, and Gaherin pledged to try to get the owners to agree. Gaherin believed Seitz was leaning toward striking the reserve clause and granting unrestricted free agency to players who played out their contracts. He encouraged the owners to negotiate limited free agency.

Most of the teams' representatives, including Reds president Bob Howsam and Cardinals owner Gussie Busch, rejected Gaherin's advice. Busch shouted at Gaherin, "You want to give away this industry. Bullshit, bullshit!" The majority of owners, with Kuhn conspicuously silent, directed Gaherin to ask Seitz for his decision. Two days before Christmas 1975, Seitz II was announced: Messersmith and McNally were unrestricted free agents. Every player had the right to play out his contract and walk. On the basis of Seitz's decision, the reserve clause was illegal.

After the Seitz II decision, the reserve clause system was replaced by free agency, and the owners had to negotiate with player agents to limit players' newfound freedom after their contracts expired. The owners were scared by the decision because they lost their absolute control over salaries unless they illegally conspired not to compete for free agents.

The owners immediately went to court over Seitz II and locked the players out of 1976 spring training. However, a federal appeals court in St. Louis upheld Seitz II on March 10, and soon spring training camps reopened. The union and teams had to negotiate a new labor agreement, but both sides agreed to start the season without a deal in hopes they could find common ground.

Miller was a reasonable, skillful negotiator. He recognized some merit to the owners' concerns and educated the players about the pros and cons of unrestricted free agency. He convinced the union membership to compromise and give the teams something they did not have at the moment: restricted free agency whereby players could not become free agents until after six seasons. Miller understood that unrestricted free agency could flood the market, and he thought most players would be better off if only a limited number of quality players were part of the bidding wars that would ensue. Miller recognized that only the best players play more than six years, so they would be the focus of owners' competition. Gaherin and Miller cut a deal in line with Miller's thinking about free agency, and the 1976 season continued without a work stoppage.

Whether the owners understood what Miller thought is not known, but the hard-line owners wanted more compensation for losing a player. They saw the 1976 negotiations as a win for the players, because Gaherin accepted a deal that recognized some free agency rights. The union and its players, on the other hand, believed the teams had won something they did not have with Seitz II in that the union had compromised and agreed to limits on players' freedom. Miller's strategy was masterful because it had the appearance of a concession yet was better for the players in the long run.

The 1976 agreement expired after the 1979 season. Even with restricted free agency, player salaries had soared. From the advent of free agency until 1980, pay had increased from an average of $46,000 to $113,000, roughly 150 percent, a sign to the teams that the system was out of control. To players, the increase proved that salaries had been artificially low under the old system.

Even though the 1976 negotiations afforded players only limited freedom, the teams decided they needed to draw a line in the sand. They were not willing to yield additional ground. The players, meanwhile, were united in their belief that they had already compromised, and the union threatened to call a strike during the season.

Ray Grebey was hired by MLB to counter Miller in the 1980 negotiations, replacing Gaherin. Gaherin was viewed by many owners as having been too soft. Also, while Miller and Gaherin respected each other, many owners harbored a personal dislike for Miller. (Some of the hostility was likely born out of anti-Semitism.) It was time for someone to beat Miller and force him to make further modifications to free agency.

Grebey was a tough labor negotiator who was known to be hostile to workers. As a corporate labor lawyer, he had a long track record of battling steelworkers and electrical workers. Grebey was selected because of his "take it or leave it" approach at General Electric, where he was the lead negotiator in a series of bitter labor disputes. The owners believed Grebey could out-negotiate Miller and put an end to what they saw as the longest winning streak in the history of baseball: the victories of the players' union. They deduced that even if they took a hard stand, the players would not strike in 1980 because with their elevated salaries, they had more to lose by not playing.

The owners served notice on October 30, 1979, as required by the expiring contract, that they would be terminating the collective bargaining agreement on December 31. This notice gained the undivided attention of the players and their union. Furthermore, when the teams purchased strike insurance for 1980, Miller and the players believed the owners wanted a strike in 1980 to break the union. When a veteran player pointed out to Grebey in early 1980 that "We gave last time," Grebey replied, "That was last time."

As negotiations continued through spring training, a number of competing proposals were exchanged, including one that the teams eventually dropped—a salary scale. But the major fight was over "direct compensation." Under the 1976 agreement, a club that signed a free agent had only to provide the former team a draft pick in the following June's amateur draft. This compensation to the former team was not a big obstacle to a club wanting to sign a star. Now, the owners wanted a much more significant deterrent. If a team signed a player deemed to be a "quality" free agent, it would need to provide a major league player to the team that lost the free agent.

The union response was swift: unless you can show us data that free agency has hurt baseball and diminished your financial position, the answer is no. The owners refused to provide that data and pushed back by claiming broadly that free agency would hurt the game in the future. The teams' obstinacy about financial disclosure was their Achilles' heel; they cried poverty, but they would not open their books. And, if they thought the players would bend, they were mistaken. Bob Boone, a player whom the owners viewed as reasonable—in contrast to the intractable Miller—summed up the players' reaction:

> They [the owners] want to raise the Titanic—we sunk that fucker and we won't sell out any player. This [direct compensation] is the main issue. Let's make sure this information gets passed along to the players—so they understand the facts. This is the battle line. All players must know why we have to hold this line.

Different players had separate concerns. Some thought the minimum salary was important, while others thought the key consideration was the service time in the big leagues needed to become eligible for salary arbitration (three years) and/or free agency (six years). Given these competing interests, Miller decided to adopt a strategy of educating the players on the long-term value of free agency without requiring additional compensation for teams beyond the draft pick. He asserted that the further compensation owners were seeking would significantly diminish salaries in the future. Players who were star free agents would see the market diminish if a team had to give up another major league player in order to sign them.

As spring training unfolded in March 1980, the negotiations stalled. Players began to distrust Grebey even more, and Miller believed the teams were trying to provoke a strike. The union had decided not to strike before spring training or during the World Series after all the players would already have been paid. But at a meeting on April 1, with the regular season set to start a week later, a subcommittee of players met to discuss a date when they would strike should that prove necessary. All of them were at different stages of their careers, with varying personal interests: Don Baylor, Mark Belanger, Bob Boone, Doug DeCinces, Phil Garner, Reggie Jackson, Randy Jones, and Mike Marshall.

At the urging of the subcommittee, the union voted in favor of a twofold strike strategy: strike soon at the end of the exhibition season, resume playing on Opening Day, and then strike during the season on May 23. The subcommittee decided on this approach "to hurt them [the owners] the most and benefit us the most." There were only a few spring training games left, but cancellation of the much-touted exhibition "Freeway Series" in Los Angeles would garner headlines. Indeed, the vote did attract attention and even outrage from sportswriters and baseball fans, but the heat on the union cooled as the brief work stoppage ended and the regular season commenced. Baseball fans and baseball writers largely sided with the owners. They saw the players as overcompensated for playing a game.

Jim Murray, a respected sportswriter for the *Los Angeles Times* and a member of the National Sportscasters and Sportswriters Association Hall of Fame, growled at the players. He was known for his sense of humor and his ability to turn a phrase, once writing that Oakland A's star outfielder Rickey Henderson "has a strike zone the size of Hitler's heart." Murray's columns were nationally syndicated, and he was popular with baseball fans.

When it appeared that a strike was likely to occur, Murray wrote columns on April 3 and May 23 that sided completely with the owners. He believed that whether a team was entitled to compensation when one of its stars was signed as a free agent by another club "is not a proper subject for a strike." He declared that baseball was not work, and that the players were "highly paid parts of an activity which contributes nothing to the gross national product except popcorn sales, whose skills were not transferable to anything that mattered. Some guys make more money than they can count..." He sarcastically urged "baseball players of the world unite! You have nothing to lose but half a million dollars—or your wife's new Rolls [Royce]."

Murray then took aim at the union and its executive director, Marvin Miller:

The craven way baseball players have gone about their strike is hardly in the best traditions of the United Mine Workers, anyway. They struck during the exhibition season, a period in which the players receive only meal money and expenses. They propose to stage the real strike sometime at the end of May, at which time I expect a vote will be somewhat less unanimous than a 767 to 1 [vote] announced for March ... [Players] were lucky baseball's around to keep them in minks and Rolls ... They should be grateful for the spadework done by generations of promoters, reporters, announcers, technicians, contractors and so forth who made it all possible. They're grateful to a man who had nothing to do with it, Marvin Miller, the only labor leader in history to represent a company of millionaires.

Most sportswriters around the country agreed. Murray's columns likely influenced any owners who were wavering about their strategy and may have emboldened them to hold firm and allow a strike to happen. While fans trusted that Murray knew what he was talking about, the players ignored his advice not to strike. They believed the union had already compromised in 1976 and was rightly protecting the gains they had achieved. They also felt they were entitled to their fair share of the revenue owners raked in because of their play on the field. As they saw it, the ticket-buying public came to see the players perform, not the owners.

Murray's view was not universal, however. Red Smith was also a nationally syndicated sportswriter who wrote four columns a week for *The New York Times*, and he sided with the union. Four years earlier, Smith had become only the second sportswriter to win the Pulitzer Prize for commentary. In recognition for having written columns for over 50 years, Smith received the J. G. Taylor Spink Award from the National Baseball Hall of Fame in 1976, the sport's highest honor for newspaper sportswriters.

Smith groused that the fans and the press were being duped by the teams into thinking the players were now asking for additional gains after the union had made its concessions in 1976. He argued that the public was gullible and that it "buys the greedy player argument blindly." Smith contended the players should not be criticized by the press and fans for accepting what was being offered to them by the owners themselves, whom Smith described as being "unable to control their own impulsive generosity... [and] are demanding that the players control it for them." If fans had the opportunity to earn more in their jobs, would they not try to do so?

Smith agreed with Miller that the owners were trying to provoke a strike. He gave his readers a brief history of baseball's labor relations before free agency when a "ballplayer was owned outright by the first club that signed him to a contract," and explained why the players were united: "All ballplayers have to strike for is the limited freedom, the self-respect and the money they have fought for and won in recent years. The employers have made no secret of their determination to diminish these gains."

Negotiations continued. With a strike looming mid-season, it became clear that a strike could be averted if the players relented on the compensation demand of the owners, which was designed to weaken free agency. The union, though, had drawn a line in the sand, and it was not budging. After Grebey wrote an article in *The Sporting News* (the premier baseball publication at the time) addressed to the players with the headline, "Grebey: Pay Averaging $149,000, Why Strike?", the players answered, practically in unison. They weren't looking for new concessions; they simply wanted to maintain the status quo. Grebey's strategy of telling the players how they should think backfired, much like similar strategies owners had tried over the past 20 years. The players joked that Grebey's letter should have been addressed to the teams, because they were the ones asking for a giveback from the union. The owners wanted a strike, not the players.

With the union's strike date of May 23 looming, Grebey and Miller continued to negotiate, seemingly in vain. On the evening of May 22, many MLB players were scheduled to board planes to go to the site of their next game. When club officials asked why players weren't showing up at their respective airports, they quickly learned that the strike was no longer an abstract idea. The players were staying home. Suddenly, Grebey presented Miller with a proposal that would allow the 1980 season to continue: the owners would establish a joint study committee to look at possible changes in the free agency system in exchange for the union dropping its less-important demands. Miller called off the strike and agreed to the proposal, as it was a way to maintain the status quo while the compensation issue was being studied by representatives from both sides.

But things took a sour turn when Grebey attempted to claim victory. He issued a public statement that erroneously claimed, "In 1981, the Clubs' proposal for compensation becomes a part of the Basic Agreement and it cannot be removed without agreement of the two sides."

This misrepresentation solidified the players' distrust of Grebey. Miller told the players that "there can be no change in compensation for free agents without the agreement of the Players Association." He called Grebey's statement "propaganda" and said that the union retained its right to strike in 1981.

Star player Don Baylor summed up the players' feelings: "I got to see Grebey close up and personal. I can only speak for myself, but my dislike of Grebey was instant and complete. Grebey was a labor gunslinger with a history of overseeing protracted strikes."

With the strike averted, the season continued, but the main issue was not resolved. The Philadelphia Phillies won the World Series in October, the franchise's first-ever world championship. The team's stars were Mike Schmidt, a product of their farm system; Steve Carlton, acquired in a trade with the St. Louis Cardinals after he requested more money; and Pete Rose, signed as a free agent when the Reds thought he insisted on too much money. Interest in Major League Baseball was at an all-time high, and free agency had resulted in heightened competition on the field.

After the season, the joint study committee convened. The players demanded solid evidence from the teams that a change was needed, along with proof that any change would benefit the players. It was a recipe for disaster, because there was no such evidence, only speculation by the owners. Meanwhile, the Yankees signed veteran Dave Winfield to a 10-year, $20-million contract. With the teams unwilling to back up their claims of financial hardships, the signing of Winfield reinforced the players' belief that the owners were lying.

In February 1981, the committee had not been able to reach a deal, and the teams unilaterally implemented their compensation proposal for teams that lost a "quality" free agent. The losing team would be compensated by the acquiring team with a major league player. The owners then mailed a letter to each player telling them that their proposal was not a salary cap like the National Football League had with its players' union (failing to mention that the NFL union was notoriously weak). The letter went on to say that the plan "is not a salary cutting effort, regardless of what some have said ... Salaries [are] at an all-time high ... The benefits of being a major-league player are at an all-time high." The players viewed the letter as a threat that they could lose a lot of money in a strike, but it also reminded them of how much they had gained because of the resolve of their union.

With the issue of team compensation still unresolved, spring training camps opened with storm clouds hanging overhead for a second straight season. The players were convinced that the teams were testing their resolve, and many accused the owners of having the surreptitious motive of breaking the union. For his part, Marvin Miller told the players bluntly that the owners could not be trusted. On February 25, the union's executive board met in Tampa, Florida, and voted 29-0 to set a May 29 strike date.

Both sides knew they could not kick the can into the next season (1982) as Grebey had done by forestalling a strike in 1980. The free agency battle hovered over the sport like a Category 5 hurricane blowing over tropical waters.

Most baseball fans, meanwhile, looked forward to a new season with the eternal hope that their team would win the 1981 World Series. The players, they thought, made too much money to be willing to disrupt the season. Oh, how they were wrong.

> "I think you boys need someone who is familiar with the courthouse."

GEORGE WRIGHT
CLASS ACTION LAWYER

5
Help Wanted

AT PRECISELY 5:00 P.M. ON FRIDAY, Far's phone rang, rousing him suddenly from a nap on his couch. "Hello," Far said. "Mr. Far, this is Buck Weaver, from Judge Jackson's courtroom. I am calling you to inform you that your motion for a TRO will be heard Monday morning. The judge requests that any additional pleadings be filed by 5:00 p.m. Sunday in our night drop box. We are informing the lawyers representing Major League Baseball and its teams of the same. Any questions?"

Suddenly, fear entered Far's mind. *Any questions? Shit, what do I know?* "Thanks, Mr. Weaver, no questions. See you Monday." Far hung up, threw on his jeans and drove to Mehlman's, where Smack and Queen were hanging out for happy hour. "Hey guys, I got the call. We are up to bat Monday morning." His friends looked at him as if they were seeing a ghost.

Once the lawsuit was filed, it became obvious that the students were in over their heads. WBNS-TV in Columbus made the lawsuit its lead story in its "breaking news" features that evening. CBS mentioned it near the end of its national news broadcast, with anchor Dan Rather smirking as he gave the news: "If you thought the revamped baseball playoffs are starting next week, think again. A class action lawsuit was filed today by three baseball fans in Ohio asking for the playoffs to be halted. We reached out to the fans and Major League Baseball, but we received no reply by the time we came on the air. A hearing is scheduled for Monday morning. Stay tuned!"

Smack looked at Far: "Dan Rather called and you did not pick up? That's ballsy."

Far laughed, "He didn't have Mehlman's number."

There was still hope that the Reds could qualify for the playoffs under the fabricated split-season rules, but hope slipped away as the Reds lost a critical game that night. It became increasingly unlikely that the dream comeback that would make their suit unnecessary was going to happen. Far, Smack, and Queen stumbled out of Mehlman's shortly after midnight knowing their mission was urgent.

Other media outlets left messages on Far's answering machine all evening. He had no idea whether to return the calls or what to say if he did, so the three students agreed to ignore them. Their mailboxes at the law school were filled with notes of encouragement, but the dean of The Ohio State University College of Law thought the three students were embarrassing the school. Dean Gregory Donald called each one Saturday and instructed them to appear in his office Monday morning. Each agreed to the dean's summons before remembering that they would all be in federal court at the time. Queen got a call from a lawyer in Cincinnati who had offered him a full-time job after graduation and told him the firm was reconsidering its offer. "Do you have any idea what you are doing? This could be embarrassing to us because we represent the Reds."

Dazed and gobsmacked with the seriousness of the matter, the boys decided they needed a real lawyer. But who? Smack volunteered to research class action lawyers and report back. By mid-afternoon Saturday, he called Far and said, "This may be crazy, but I think I found the right guy. He's in Cincinnati and is known as the 'master of disaster' because he takes on huge corporations."

"Who is that?" asked Far.

"His name is George Wright," Smack replied. Far laughed to himself but did not explain anything further to Smack.

"I will call him," said Far. You think I can reach him on a Saturday? I hope he's in his office."

Sure enough, when Far called the Cincinnati lawyer, an answering service picked up. "Chase and Wright, may I help you?"

Far stumbled. "Yes, Mr. Wright, please." After being on hold for several minutes, a voice came on.

"Hello, this is George Wright." Far knew of Wright when his name was mentioned by Smack. Wright was a distant relative of Harry Wright, known as the "father of baseball" in America and the manager of the first professional baseball team, the 1869 Cincinnati Red Stockings. Far had an inkling that the case would appeal to a man with Wright's heritage, but were they reaching out to him too late?

Far described what they had done the day before, and Wright said he had read a small piece in *The Cincinnati Enquirer* that morning. He was intrigued. "I think you boys need someone who is familiar with the courthouse. Who's the judge?" When Far told Wright it was Jackson, Wright said, "He's a good man. He was once falsely accused of cheating when he played semipro ball, and he won't like it if he thinks baseball is cheating the fans. He hates hypocrites. You might have a chance, but you have to understand what you are up against. MLB is the epitome of corporate America. This is a long shot, but you'll learn a lot about the law in just a couple of days. And if the Reds lose tonight, we will know they definitely need us. They could be eliminated from this bullshit second-half pennant race by midnight."

Wright had not inherited the baseball talent of his great-grandfather, but he was a rabid baseball fan, and he too was upset with MLB owners, Commissioner Kuhn, and, to a lesser extent, the players' union. "My great-grandfather is tossing and turning in his grave. He would be sick over how money has taken over the game, and that's what this is all about." (The statement was ironic because his great-grandfather was actually the first owner to pay all of his players and recognize the team as a professional baseball squad.)

Far assured Wright they had done all the factual research supporting their legal claim, and that they had smarter classmates from the law journal volunteering to research relevant precedent. They promised to get Wright up to speed if he could come to Columbus, and they even offered to reimburse his travel expenses.

Wright agreed to go the distance with the young law students. He arranged for one of his private planes to fly him from Cincinnati to Columbus early Sunday morning. Wright and "the boys"' (as Wright called them) met at Mehlman's precisely at 9:00 a.m. on Sunday. Wright exited the limo that he had arranged at the airport, and he was accompanied by two others who looked like bodyguards, flanking his sides. "Boys, I brought a couple of experienced lawyers with me, Mr. Chase and Mr. DeMarco, as well as three paralegals, Ed Cicotte, Lefty Williams, and Swede Risberg. They all know baseball history very well. Do you mind?" Mind? Far, Smack, and Queen were relieved! Maybe these guys know what they are doing.

Mehlman's was a frequent stop for the boys, and the owners—Eileen "Happy" Felsch and Fred "Opey" McMullen—practically considered them their kids. The boys had taken over the back half of Mehlman's earlier that morning. They downed a couple shots of Dewar's Scotch to loosen up and spread out their 24 boxes on 15 tables. The lawyers, paralegals, and students got down to business quickly, with Queen explaining the contents of each box. Seventy-five minutes later, Wright remarked, "That is impressive work. Let's get working on a summary that we can file today by the deadline," he said. "Jackson needs to know our best arguments before he sees us in the morning. The Reds were officially eliminated last night, so we know the case is alive."

Chase took the lead. He had once been called "The Black Prince of Baseball" for gambling on minor league games as a player but was never suspended. "I get the argument. Let me start typing. Why don't you guys put stickers on those boxes and we will make them our exhibits. Label them 1 through 24. With that, Chase pulled out a roll of blue stickers labeled "Plaintiff's Exhibit __" for the boys to use.

"DeMarco," directed Wright, "start scribbling your argument on the motion to dismiss we will probably see, and Chase, can you find what I need in the boxes while I type?" Three hours later, Wright had prepared a 23-page memorandum labeled "Plaintiffs' Summary Argument in Favor of a Temporary Restraining Order."

Chase and DeMarco proofed Wright's work, finding just a few typos that were quickly fixed with correction fluid. With the memo good to go, Chase handed it to Far, saying "Make 50 copies down the street at that copy shop, and slide 10 into the night drop box at the courthouse. Hurry! If we are late, the court may disregard it."

Far scurried out of Mehlman's to a nearby copy shop, leaving behind his old and new friends thirsting for another beer or two. When Far returned just before 5:00 p.m., Wright told the boys, "Well done. Now, let's get a good night's sleep. It will be a long day tomorrow. Let's meet here at 8:00

a.m. and walk to the courthouse. Nothing like a good night's sleep to prepare for an oral argument."

Felsch and McMullen had been eavesdropping. "We will open up early. This is historic. Kuhn really ruined a fantastic season. I even went to Opening Day this year. I don't think I will next year. We don't like hypocrites. See you at 8:00 a.m."

Historical markers define April 1981, and a less-heralded member of the Great Eight shines bright.

6
A Season Unlike Any Other Begins

DESPITE THE SIMMERING LABOR ISSUE, Reds fans were hopeful as 1981 approached. After finishing just 3.5 games out of the 1980 playoffs, they were confident in the pitching rotation anchored by Seaver and young stud Mario Soto. In addition, the remaining Big Red Machine regulars (Bench, Concepción, Foster, and Griffey) were buttressed by solid role players Dan Driessen, Ray Knight, Dave Collins, and Ron Oester. And with the Reds under new ownership, there were plenty of reasons for optimism.

Shortly after Ronald Reagan became president in January, brothers William and James Williams purchased stock in the Reds from Louis Nippert and became principal owners of the team. After promising fans a return to glory, the brothers soon arranged for the first pitch to be delivered by Reagan. It was an honor for the city, as no sitting president had ever thrown out the first pitch at an opener in Cincinnati, the only city given the honor each year of hosting Opening Day.

Adding to the excitement of Reagan's attendance was the anticipation of a pitching matchup made in Cooperstown. Seaver was scheduled to face

Steve Carlton of the Phillies. Never before had two more distinguished pitchers opened the season in Cincinnati. (Hall of Fame pitchers Eppa Rixey for the Reds and Grover Cleveland Alexander for the Chicago Cubs faced off in the 1922 opener, but they were in the middle of their careers and were not yet as accomplished.) "It's great for the fans, but I don't like to think about it that way. I'm not pitching against Carlton. I'm pitching against the Phillies," said Seaver.

Tickets were sold out early in the winter, but history intervened to derail Reagan's visit. On March 30, John Hinckley Jr. shot Reagan as he was leaving the Hilton Hotel in Washington, D.C. Secret Service agent Timothy McCarthy hurled himself in the line of fire between the gunman and Reagan, and the agent's willingness to absorb the bullet likely saved the president's life. Two days later, the White House announced that Reagan would not be well enough to make an appearance in Cincinnati for the April 8 opener.

Supreme Court Justice Potter Stewart, a Cincinnati native, was in his hometown on the eve of the opener. He was there to attend a ceremony for the formal unveiling of his portrait that would hang in the main courtroom of the federal Sixth Circuit Court of Appeals located next to Fountain Square. (Later, the courthouse would be named in his honor.) Stewart acknowledged that the assassination attempt was traumatic, but he also reminded his audience that it was a "tremendous unifying event" for the country. *The Cincinnati Enquirer* noted the gravity of the assassination attempt with the headline, "This Opening Day Has a Dark Cloud on the Horizon." At the opener, fans wore sweatshirts bearing the message "Together We Can" while wondering who would replace Reagan in making the ceremonial first pitch. As the first pitch was about to take place, 30-year Reds public-address announcer Paul Sommerkamp introduced the Roger Bacon High School band as they played their signature tune, "This

Is My Country." Sommerkamp then made a somber announcement:

> Ladies and gentlemen, had certain events of nine days ago not taken place we would be honored to introduce to you a very good baseball fan who was to have thrown out our ceremonial first pitch... He is not here today in person, but we are sure he is with us in spirit. Ladies and gentlemen, there can really be no appropriate relief pitcher for the President of the United States and we have decided that it is most appropriate in 1981 to have no ceremonial pitcher.

He then asked the crowd to observe a moment of silence "as we give thanks for the physical recovery of Ronald Reagan." Sommerkamp almost choked up at the end of his announcement.

The Seaver-Carlton matchup lived up to its hype, as each hurler surrendered just one run. The Reds won a thriller in the bottom of the ninth, 3-2. The locals were pleased to see Oester, a Cincinnati native, making his first-ever appearance in an Opening Day game. He had been on the team since 1978 but had never appeared in an opener. This year, he started at second base. Oester defied the odds and fulfilled the dreams of many young ball players from Cincinnati. He went to his first Opening Day game at the age of 12 at iconic Crosley Field and vowed to become a major leaguer. Twelve years later, he was starting for the home team on Opening Day. Oester confirmed what native Cincinnatians knew:

> It's really a holiday... Here, the people go crazy. I know a lot of people take off work for the game. I remember my friends taking radios to school on Opening Day so we could listen to the game. I skipped class in grade school a couple of years to stay home and watch the game on television. My parents let me do it. It's a really special day.

Oester went hitless, but the thrill of playing that day was the fulfillment of his lifelong dream.

Cincinnati embarked on a six-day road trip after Opening Day, dropping two out of three in Atlanta but then recovering to sweep the Padres in San Diego. In the finale versus the Friars, the Reds scored all 10 of their runs in the final four innings. Driessen, Perez's replacement, clubbed a three-run home run and drove in four, and Soto, building off his breakout 1980 season, tossed a one-run, complete-game shutout. Mini-streaks defined the rest of the Reds' April: a four-game losing streak at home (two to St. Louis, two to Atlanta); a sweep of the Astros in Houston; and a three-game thrashing of San Diego at Riverfront during which the hosts outscored the visitors 23-10. Cincinnati had started the season strong, finishing April with an 11-7 record.

One of the historic achievements of the month belonged to Seaver, who became the fifth member of the 3,000-strikeout club on April 18 during the Reds' 10-4 defeat of the Cardinals. Seaver wasn't exactly beaming with pride following his notable achievement, dubbing the pitch that completed his final strikeout "a lousy high slider." Tom Terrific may not have had his best stuff on his memorable day—the righty allowed four runs (one earned) on six hits over five innings—but 1981 was the 1992 Hall of Fame inductee's last great season. Seaver's 14 wins led the majors, and he just missed procuring his fourth Cy Young Award, falling two percentage points short (58% to 56%) in the voting to the Dodgers' rookie sensation, Fernando Valenzuela.

Concepción, one of the Machine's old gears, was named NL Player of the Month in April, racking up an impressive slash line (batting average .364/on-base percentage .436/slugging percentage .576) along with 21 RBI in 18 games. In Cincinnati's penultimate game of April, Concepción, immersed in year 12 of an eventual 19-year-sojourn with the franchise, smacked two home runs, the lone round-trippers the shortstop would hit all month.

A native Venezuelan, Dave Concepción played for a local amateur team after attending high school. Fortunately for the Reds, the coach of that team was Wilfredo Calvino, who doubled as a scout for Cincinnati. Concepción signed with the Reds in September 1967 and required just two seasons in the minors, including a 42-game stint in 1969 at Triple-A Indianapolis, where the lanky shortstop hit .342. He earned his place as the Reds' starting shortstop on Opening Day in 1970 at age 21.

Though he eventually became known for his fielding prowess, it was Concepción's glove that prevented him from locking down the starting shortstop position in his first major league season. By mid-June, he had made 14 errors and was replaced by Woody Woodward. Concepción eventually regained some playing time and hit .260 in 101 games. When Cincinnati reached the postseason (and the World Series) for the first time in nine years in 1970, Concepción started the final three games of the World Series and picked up three hits in 10 plate appearances.

Concepción really struggled at the plate in 1971 (.205 average in 130 games) and 1972 (.209 in 119 games). His propensity for errors remained an issue, though defensive metrics rate him as an above-average or excellent defensive shortstop for nearly his entire career.

Concepción broke through in 1973 and made the All-Star team for the first time, but his season was cut short after suffering a leg injury in late July. He was hitting .287 at the time. Through the rest of the decade, Concepción played in at least 140 games for the Big Red Machine. From 1974 to 1977, he was the NL Gold Glove winner at shortstop. He earned the distinction of stealing 20 or more bases in six straight years, including 41 in 1974. In 1979,

> Concepción hit a career-best 16 home runs and drove in 84 runs. Forever overshadowed by some of his Big Red Machine teammates and underappreciated for his sheer consistency, Concepción garnered the seventh of what would be eight consecutive All-Star nods in 1981.
> He went on to finish fourth in the MVP voting, one spot behind Foster.

At 11-7, Cincinnati was 2.5 games back of the 14-5 Dodgers in the NL West on April 30. Los Angeles had been buoyed by the sudden emergence of Valenzuela, a 20-year-old left-handed pitcher signed out of Mexico less than two years earlier. Valenzuela, who had pitched in 10 games for the Dodgers in 1980 in relief, made his first career start on Opening Day against Houston and promptly shut out the defending NL West champs over nine innings, striking out five. Valenzuela had only started because of an injury to two-time All-Star Jerry Reuss.

Surely the rival Giants would fare better against Valenzuela in the rookie's next start, right? Nope. Valenzuela allowed a single run and fanned 10 over nine innings. Valenzuela started three more games in April, completing 27 innings, allowing zero runs, and earning 28 strikeouts. Throw in his funky delivery and his wacky screwball, and "Fernandomania" was born.

Over the pitching prodigy's initial eight starts, he registered an ERA of 0.50. Valenzuela struck out 68 over 72 innings, and Los Angeles won all eight of his starts. Valenzuela was truly a phenomenon, amassing a cult following, particularly among fans of Latin descent. Eleven of Valenzuela's first 12 home starts were sellouts. Before 1981, the Dodgers had broken the 3 million attendance mark only two times. From 1982 to 1986, the franchise eclipsed 3 million in each season, and in 1982 established a new MLB attendance record with 3.6 million fans.

Valenzuela went on to pitch 11 seasons (1980 through 1990) for the Dodgers, winning 141 games and picking up six All-Star appearances. But, arguably, even in a shortened season, 1981 was Valenzuela's pièce de résistance. He led the league in starts, complete games, innings pitched, shutouts, and strikeouts. Valenzuela's 2.48 ERA was nothing to sneeze at either; the precocious southpaw became the first pitcher ever to win both Rookie of the Year and the Cy Young Award in the same year. Not bad for a 20-year-old.

In the NL East, Steve Carlton not only lost his titanic matchup with Seaver on Opening Day, he also was 11 days behind Seaver in recording his 3,000th strikeout. By one measure, Carlton's admission to baseball's most noteworthy strikeout club was perhaps more significant than Seaver's, as the southpaw was the first left-handed pitcher in history to reach the milestone. Carlton's 3,000th strikeout occurred in the first inning of the 6-2 Phillies' victory against the Montreal Expos on April 29. The 36-year-old struck out Tim Raines, Jerry Manuel, and Tim Wallach to reach an even 3,000 strikeouts. Thirty-eight more years—nearly to the day—would pass before another lefty, CC Sabathia, entered the 3,000-strikeout club on April 30, 2019. Carlton tossed nine innings and fanned nine in his famed start, his fourth complete game of the month, including one 10-inning showing. He threw four more complete games in May and went on to log another impressive season in Philadelphia, striking out 179 in 190 innings and attaining a 2.42 ERA. Like Seaver, Carlton's chances for a fourth Cy Young award were dashed by Valenzuela, with Carlton finishing a relatively distant third in the voting.

Though the Expos may have been on the wrong end of Carlton's big night, with a 12-4 record, they were kings of the National League East through April. St. Louis (9-3) and Philadelphia (12-6) sat just a single game back, though. In the American League, Oakland (18-3) raced to a five-game lead over the Chicago White Sox (11-6) on the strength of an incredible 11-0 start. In the East, the Yankees (11-6) were a half-game in front of Cleveland (8-4) and 1.5 games ahead of Milwaukee (9-7).

Weather factored heavily into teams' early-season records, because some teams largely escaped bad weather while others saw frequent rainouts. For example, San Francisco played 21 games between the start of the season on April 9 and April 30. San Diego suited up 20 times. In contrast, St. Louis and Pittsburgh played only 12 and 13 contests, respectively, during that time.

In the American League, both Oakland and California completed 21 games, while Cleveland played 12 games and Kansas City 13. For the American League, which had 14 franchises compared with the National League's 12, the median number of games played by a team in April was 16.5, with the average at 16.9. In the National League, the median was 18.0 and the average was 17.0. The disparity in games played seemed innocuous at the time, since games are typically made up during the course of a normal 162-game season. But in the madness of 1981, the discrepancy in games played wound up being a major reference point in the unfairness of the season.

NL WEST STANDINGS THROUGH APRIL					
Team	Wins	Losses	Ties	W/L %	Games Back
Los Angeles Dodgers	14	5	0	.737	–
Cincinnati Reds	11	7	0	.611	2.5
Atlanta Braves	9	10	0	.474	5.0
San Francisco Giants	9	12	0	.429	6.0
Houston Astros	7	12	0	.368	7.0
San Diego Padres	6	14	0	.300	8.5

NL EAST STANDINGS THROUGH APRIL

Team	Wins	Losses	Ties	W/L %	Games Back
Montreal Expos	12	4	0	.750	--
St. Louis Cardinals	9	3	1	.750	1.0
Philadelphia Phillies	12	6	0	.667	1.0
Pittsburgh Pirates	7	6	1	.538	3.5
New York Mets	4	10	1	.286	7.0
Chicago Cubs	2	13	1	.133	9.5

AL WEST STANDINGS THROUGH APRIL

Team	Wins	Losses	Ties	W/L %	Games Back
Oakland Athletics	18	3	0	.857	--
Chicago White Sox	11	6	0	.647	5.0
Texas Rangers	10	7	0	.588	6.0
California Angels	10	11	0	.476	8.0
Minnesota Twins	6	12	1	.333	10.5
Kansas City Royals	3	10	0	.231	11.0
Seattle Mariners	5	14	1	.263	12.0

AL EAST STANDINGS THROUGH APRIL

Team	Wins	Losses	Ties	W/L %	Games Back
New York Yankees	11	6	0	.647	--
Cleveland Indians	8	4	0	.667	0.5
Milwaukee Brewers	9	7	0	.563	1.5
Baltimore Orioles	7	8	0	.467	3.0
Boston Red Sox	7	9	0	.438	3.5
Detroit Tigers	8	11	0	.421	4.0
Toronto Blue Jays	7	12	0	.368	5.0

> "We will provide continuous live coverage of the trial as developments warrant."

GEORGE GRANDE
ESPN ANCHOR

7

The Media Descends on Columbus

OCTOBER 5, 9:00 AM

THE FEDERAL COURTROOM IN COLUMBUS, OHIO, was packed like never before. Most of those in the gallery were Reds fans who descended on Ohio's capital city that morning. It reminded some veteran news reporters of the Sam Sheppard murder trial 27 years earlier in Cleveland, by far the most-watched trial in Ohio court history. The courtroom was on the second floor of the stately US Post Office and Courthouse, located on the Scioto River in Ohio's capital city.

Typical of the attendees were five students. Bill O'Conner, a student at Ohio State's dental school, recruited his four buddies from the 1976 Elder High School class—the four were enjoying their fifth years at Columbus-area colleges—to make the drive that morning. O'Conner arrived early; he was used to waking at 5:00 a.m. to begin his daily studies. Terry Finley, Tom Kneflin, Joe Sharbell, and Dan Murphy greeted him just outside the courtroom. The five were Reds die-hards—they had been to World Series games in Cincinnati while they were in grade school in 1970 and when they attended Elder High School in 1975. They were each sporting shorts and T-shirts with various Reds logos.

Outside the courthouse, rookie WLWT-Cincinnati sports reporter Larry Bill interviewed the dental student and his friends. Murphy proclaimed to the camera that "we have a five-game World Series winning streak to continue," a reference to the Reds Game 7 victory in 1975 and their four-game sweep of the Yankees the following year.

Finley chimed in, "This judge better do the right thing, but I think MLB will try to confuse him with their sanctimonious garbage about the integrity of the game."

Kneflin, taking one last smoke before entering, admitted to the reporter that "this is fun, but I'm not optimistic." O'Conner did not want the spotlight, declined an interview, and opened the front door to the federal courthouse. He signaled for his friends to enter.

Sharbell brought up the rear and stirred the pot as he liked to do. "I hope they call me as a witness, because I'd hate to see you boys under oath."

Finley remarked, "Joe you don't know shit about anything—none of us will be on the stand."

Not to be outdone, the news anchor for WCPO-TV, Al Schottelkotte, treated this as a news story. Schottelkotte was the Walter Cronkite of Cincinnati news. Naturally, he recruited a legal expert, Ron Major, to weigh in. Major was a legendary trial lawyer, known for taking on tough cases like The Who concert tragedy in Cincinnati a few years earlier, and was liked by local news media pining for legal analysis. Schottelkotte questioned Major live on the "Breaking News" segment that interrupted local programming. "Mr. Major, this seems like a publicity stunt, agreed?"

Major fought back. "No law student in their right mind would bring this suit unless they had really researched this. They are putting their law careers at risk. Reviewing what they have written, I see no reason why justice will not prevail. The court, after all, is supposed to ensure justice, and who can argue that the Reds don't belong in the postseason?"

Over a hundred angry fans with placards and signs squeezed onto 20 benches behind the bar separating the gallery from the lawyers. O'Conner's posse managed to cram into the second row. There were hundreds of others protesting outside because they could not be accommodated in the courtroom. Marconi Boulevard in front of the courthouse was shut down to traffic, and the Columbus police department chose not to bother the protesters. After all, the police were Reds fans, even though Columbus was a two-team town. While fans of the Big Red Machine predominated, some Columbus residents supported the Triple-A affiliate of the Cleveland Indians (renamed the Cleveland Guardians in 2021).

The most interested parties in the courthouse that day—besides the fans and owners—were ABC Sports and NBC Sports. The networks had a total of 10 executives in the first row, mostly vice presidents of sales who were concerned about the possible loss of advertising revenue if any playoff games were canceled. They were used to the uncertainty of how long playoff series would last, because it was always anybody's guess as to whether they would get a four-game sweep or a seven-game barn burner in the World Series. The number of games mattered greatly to them, as every game played in the postseason brought in top-dollar advertising revenue.

The next afternoon, ABC was set to air the first game in MLB's "Division Series Playoffs," the additional round of four three-game series added to the postseason by Bowie Kuhn. ABC and NBC planned to televise the two leagues' five-game Championship Series that would follow the divisional battles, and ABC had the rights to the World Series, which could go to seven games. The networks were eager to recoup the ad revenue they lost from the games missed during the summer, whether because of the strike or rainouts, but the games had to take place in order for them to be paid. If the law students' injunction prevailed, their chances of earning top dollar would be thwarted.

John Bogusz, ABC's vice president of sales, was anxious. He had flown in the day before and met with MLB executives who were certain the case would be dismissed quickly enough that the games scheduled for Tuesday would proceed. "I don't know," thought Bogusz. "We have an Ohio judge and a region full of Reds fans who would love to see Cincinnati in the playoffs."

His intern, Jeff Betz, thought like the owners. "You're nuts. I have us on a flight back to New York this evening." Bogusz and Betz had gone to the same college, the University of Dayton, and Bogusz knew that Betz, a Cleveland native, was no Reds fan.

Betz's boss gave him a disapproving look and responded, "Jeff, I hope you got flights that are changeable, or you may be going home by yourself."

The extra playoff games created by the commissioner pitting the first-half and second-half division winners against each other would be a ratings bonanza for both networks. The games were scheduled to begin a mere 28 hours later. The networks had paid MLB tens of millions of dollars for the rights to broadcast the games, and the airtime they sold to advertisers had more than covered that cost. Advertisers were anxious to buy the rights to 30- and 60-second TV commercials for what they hoped would be the largest prime-time audience ever during the two leagues' Championship Series and then the World Series. Ironically, the labor dispute, the strike, and the ensuing controversy had kept baseball in the news throughout the year, and sales guys such as Bogusz relished the idea that casual fans would tune in precisely because of the public wrangling. And Kuhn's split-season plan had guaranteed ever since August that teams from major television markets—New York, Los Angeles, Philadelphia, and the San Francisco Bay Area—would take part in the postseason.

While the established networks were sweating out the potential loss of revenue, a nontraditional media genre was just gaining a foothold—cable television. Still in its infancy, cable television had no playoff rights, but a fledgling network called the Entertainment and Sports Programming Network, or ESPN, decided that featuring the MLB playoffs could grab much-needed eyeballs. ESPN's ratings did not even register on the national Nielsen ratings that drove advertising revenue. The network had launched on September 7, 1979, at 7:00 p.m., and only an estimated 30,000 viewers tuned in for the debut of *SportsCenter* with anchors Lee Leonard and George Grande. The first words spoken were from Leonard, who informed viewers: "If you're a fan, *if* you're a fan, what you'll see in the next minutes, hours, and days to follow may convince you you've gone to sports heaven." Early ESPN programming (other than *SportsCenter*) included men's slow-pitch softball, assorted minor college sports (not college basketball or football), boxing, and wrestling.

Stuart Evey, who controlled ESPN, called Grande as soon as the lawsuit broke on Friday. "Get on a plane to Columbus. Let's give wall-to-wall coverage of that lawsuit aiming to halt the playoffs."

Grande was stunned. "Why are we giving that nonsense any air?"

"Because there are millions of baseball fans upset with MLB, and no other network will give it much attention. It could be a ratings bonanza, which we sorely need," Evey said. "And CBS already beat us. Goddamn Rather gave it play. Make sure it's the top story tonight and then get a flight."

Grande usually sat at a desk called the "ESPN SportsCenter" to host the network's nightly sports broadcast. He also served as host of the

Inside Baseball weekly magazine program, and Grande was respected within the game. In 1980, he had even been named master of ceremonies for the National Baseball Hall of Fame's annual inductions. Grande was concerned that Kuhn and the owners would not like him covering the case, but he figured he would go to Columbus and size things up. As he told Leonard, "The lawsuit will quickly go away, and I can't just tell Stuart no. He's too concerned about our viability. See you Tuesday."

ESPN had struggled financially since its founding in 1978, but Anheuser-Busch invested $1 million in ESPN in 1980 and an additional $5 million in 1981. The brewer believed that beer drinkers were sports fans, so advertising on ESPN would be an effective way to reach the target audience. Without these capital inflows, the network likely would have folded. Evey knew that he couldn't continue to count on being propped up and that ratings needed to show marked improvement. To that end, ESPN was in talks to become a broadcast partner for the National Basketball Association, which would mark its initial entry into American professional sports. But baseball was far more popular than basketball, and Evey wanted to draw in all the baseball fans he could.

Grande arrived in Columbus on Sunday afternoon and started both the 6:00 p.m. and 11:00 p.m. *SportsCenter* broadcast by explaining the story behind the lawsuit. He told viewers, "We will provide continuous live coverage of the trial as developments warrant."

A different cable network, the Cable News Network, or CNN, was launched on June 1, 1980. CNN was the brainchild of one of MLB's newest owners, Ted Turner. Turner was nicknamed "The Mouth of the South." Born in Cincinnati in 1938, he had grown up as a Reds fan. He made his fortune by building an advertising empire, followed by forays into radio and television. Turner bought the Atlanta Braves in 1976 and the NBA Atlanta Hawks in 1977. Turner, ever brash and outspoken, quickly found himself caught in the crosshairs of Commissioner Kuhn. Like another new owner, George Steinbrenner of the Yankees, Turner saw free agency as a way to bring his team back to respectability. The Braves lost almost 100 games in both 1975 and 1976, and attendance at home was dismal, with fewer than 10,000 fans attending most games.

Turner first drew the ire of Kuhn when he signed Andy Messersmith, the winner of the landmark Seitz II decision that created free agency. He wanted Messersmith to wear "CHANNEL" on his jersey above his number, 17, to promote Turner's television station, WTBS. Kuhn nixed the uniform idea. When the Braves signed another free agent, Gary Matthews of the San Francisco Giants, to a five-year, $1.8-million contract after the 1976 season, Kuhn was irate. He suspended Turner for tampering because of remarks Turner had made about Matthews to the Giants owner during the 1976 World Series. (The suspension was later overturned.)

After the 1980 season, as MLB was selling the idea that some franchises might fold under the weight of free agency, Kuhn had publicly talked about the money Turner was losing in Atlanta—a seemingly staggering amount of $3.4 million per year. Turner certainly did not like being used as the example of irresponsible management, but he sided with Kuhn about the need for a strike. "Who believes in unions?" Turner reportedly asked at one management meeting in 1981. When no one raised a hand, Turner bellowed, "Then let's bust this one!"

The husband-and-wife team of David Walker and Lois Hart anchored CNN's first newscast and, unlike traditional television networks, CNN broadcast news 24 hours a day. They had a huge vacuum to fill, and the baseball controversy helped ratings. Turner did not discourage the coverage, as he needed CNN to bring in much-needed revenue. He sent Walker to Columbus in preparation for airing in-depth coverage of the lawsuit. Broadcasting from Columbus, Walker greeted viewers Monday morning with this opener: "You won't believe it, but Major League Baseball is being held to account in a federal courtroom today!"

In total, 28 media outlets from across the country sent reporters and artists to sketch the courtroom drama for newspapers and television news. Skeptical of the lawsuit's merit, some of the veteran sportswriters and broadcasters were nonetheless sympathetic. They knew how, after an exciting spring, most of the summer was ruined when the Boys of Summer became the Strikers of Summer.

More pitching milestones, Johnny Bench's new position and injury, and the Reds finally hit their stride.

8
A Banner First Half

THE REDS STUMBLED through the first half of May, losing seven of 10, dropping their record to 14-14. In modern times, Cincinnati's struggles versus St. Louis are well-documented. The Reds have ebbed and flowed out of phases of rebuilding and general ineptitude, while the Cardinals have reached the postseason more often than not. St. Louis managed to win the World Series in 2006 and 2011, taking Cincinnati's lunch money along the way. The gap between the two franchises was especially pronounced in 1981, as the Reds were 0-5 against the Cardinals. If five meetings between these two teams seems low despite a strike-shortened season, remember that from 1969 to 1994, Cincinnati and St. Louis were in opposite divisions: the Reds in the NL West, the Cardinals in the NL East. Cincinnati's 5-4, 11-inning loss to St. Louis on May 3 was the final time the two clubs met in the 1981 regular season.

Cincinnati recovered from its doldrums to rip off an eight-game, pitching-fueled winning streak. From May 12 to May 20, Reds pitchers surrendered just 16 runs. Mike LaCoss, who wound up with a 6.12 ERA on the season, blanked the Pirates over nine innings on May 16. Three days later, Seaver (five innings) and Paul Moskau (four innings) combined to shut out the Cubs on four hits before an announced crowd of 5,896 at Wrigley Field, dropping Chicago to 5-26.

The Cubs won the next day, after which the Reds returned home for four games versus the Dodgers. Los Angeles took three of the four games, with Dave Stewart tallying back-to-back victories in relief on May 22 and 23. The Reds were 23-18 following the series with the Dodgers and more or less held serve the rest of the month, coming in at 27-20. But before the month was over, things changed for the Reds—and certainly not for the better.

During his 17-season career, Johnny Bench played 17,713 regular-season innings. For 14,847 and two-thirds of those innings, his position was catcher. In the postseason, Bench was behind the plate for 45 games and 408 and one-third innings. By 1981, Bench's full-time catching days were over—by order of Bench himself. During the offseason, Bench informed general manager Dick Wagner that he would not continue as the team's full-time catcher. Entering the season at age 33, Bench had arthritis in both knees, had undergone an operation on his right shoulder, and suffered from back spasms and an inflamed right elbow. A catcher can take only so many crouches, collisions, and throws around the infield before it's time to hang up the mitt. "I've been shot with so many painkillers in order to stay in the lineup," Bench said in March 1981, "that if I were a race horse I'd be illegal."

In 1960, when Bench was 13, the population of his hometown of Binger, Oklahoma, was 603. It's difficult to imagine how he was even noticed by baseball scouts, let alone tracked well enough to be taken in the second round of the 1965 draft. Like Dave Concepción, Bench rocketed through the Reds' farm system, reaching Triple-A by age

18. He was named Minor League Player of the Year by *The Sporting News* in 1967. Bench was in the bigs later that year at 19, and at 20, he was an All-Star and a Gold Glove winner, the first rookie backstop to accomplish this feat. At 22, Bench was the NL MVP, with his prolific offensive and defensive capabilities redefining the catching position.

During his first MVP season in 1970, Bench led the majors with 45 home runs and 148 RBI, and he won his third straight Gold Glove, racking up a ridiculous 7.4 wins above replacement (WAR). Bench quickly became both a team leader and a celebrity, stunning veterans with his poise and confidence while also becoming a frequent guest on the talk show circuit. After another All-Star showing in 1971, Bench was MVP again in 1972, once again pacing baseball in home runs (40) and RBI (125). He collected two more top-five MVP finishes in 1974 and 1975 as the Big Red Machine flourished and Bench's penchant for timely hits drew a national audience. Bench slumped during the regular season in 1976, hitting just .234 with 16 home runs in 135 games. From 1969 to 1975, Bench had hit at least 25 home runs a season, but he was particularly magnificent during Cincinnati's dominant postseason run, especially versus the Yankees in the 1976 World Series. He hit .533 over in the four-game sweep, earning World Series MVP honors.

Bench's last great season came in 1977, when he bopped 31 homers, drove in 109 runs, and claimed the last of his 10 consecutive Gold Gloves. Bench is widely considered to be one of the top catchers to ever play the game if not the best, a contention buttressed by Bench having amassed more WAR than any other catcher in history.

Bench had experience at other positions, as he'd occasionally manned first base, third base, left field and right field throughout his career. Understandably, Bench's teammates weren't offering up their positions, and they seemingly harbored little empathy for the club legend. "No way he can play third base as well as I can. I'm not concerned," said Ray Knight.

The beat went on. "The only way he can put himself at first base is if he's the manager, and he ain't managing this team yet," said Dan Driessen.

What say you, right fielder Dave Collins? "If I stay healthy, he's not coming out here." Bench said he didn't blame any of his teammates for their candid responses. It's quite likely he would have felt the same way.

By May 27, Bench had gotten his wish ... sort of. His full-time backstop days were over, but on the days he played, he was still catching. Through April, all seven of Bench's starts were behind the plate. But when the calendar flipped to May, Bench suddenly became the club's full-time first baseman. On May 2, Driessen suffered a hand bruise after being hit by a pitch. Driessen didn't bat for over two weeks, and then he went 0-for-11 upon his return. From May 3 through May 28, Bench started 18 games—18 at first base and zero at catcher. Driessen started only four games over that stretch and grew so frustrated that he asked Wagner for a trade on May 26. At the time, Driessen was hitting .175. Out of context, the trade request may have seemed absurd, but Driessen wasn't without batting credentials; he hit .357 in the 1976 World Series and .300 in 151 games in 1977 after replacing Tony Perez at first base.

Bench, meanwhile, was thriving, hitting .333 with a .402 on-base percentage. There was no way McNamara could sit Bench now, right? Well, fate intervened on May 28 when Bench fractured his left ankle sliding into second base during a double-play break-up attempt. Driessen struggled in spite of his newfound job security, finishing the year with a .236 average and seven home runs in 82 games. His performance fell off sharply from his 1980 showing when he hit .265, logged a .377 on-base percentage, and led the National League in walks. As for Bench, the injury cost him a chance to extend his streak of successive All-Star appearances to a staggering 14. Bench would play in his 14th All-Star Game during his final season in 1983, when he was chiefly stationed at first and third base.

The league-wide pitching milestones continued into May after Seaver, Valenzuela, and Carlton grabbed the April headlines. In the second game of a doubleheader on May 10, Montreal's Charlie Lea tossed the first no-hitter in the brief history of Olympic Stadium. Neither the Expos nor the Giants cracked the scoreboard until the hosts scored four in the seventh. Lea faced the minimum through seven, then used a double play to work around a trio of eighth-inning free passes. Six days later, Lea blanked the Giants again over nine innings, though he surrendered four hits that time. Lea was named NL Pitcher of the Month after notching 29.1 consecutive scoreless innings over the course of his final four May starts.

Five days after Lea's no-no, Cleveland's Len Barker delivered the pitching masterpiece of the 1981 season, the 10th perfect game in baseball history. Barker was coming off a strong season in 1980, where he threw 246 and a third innings and struck out an American League-best 187 batters en route to 19 victories. (He also led the league with 14 wild pitches). In the three starts prior to his act of perfection, Barker had toyed with the Royals, White Sox, and Twins, yielding just two runs over 26 innings and striking out 23. On May 15, in front of an announced crowd of 7,290, Barker was solid gold in baseball's first perfect game since 1968, when Catfish Hunter beat the Twins. According to *Sports Illustrated*, the 25-year-old native of Fort Knox, Kentucky, threw just 17 fastballs after the fourth inning. "By the fifth inning his breaking ball was so good we figured that's what we'd pretty much stay with," said Cleveland catcher Ron Hassey. "By the ninth inning we decided if there was going to be a base hit, it would have to come off a breaking pitch." All 11 of Barker's strikeouts came via the swinging variety and he failed to reach a single three-ball count.

As May drew to a close, an iconic position player stole headlines. Boston's Carl Yastrzemski, who once had the impossible task of replacing Ted Williams as the Red Sox's star left fielder, played in his 3,000th game. On May 25, "Yaz" joined Ty Cobb, Stan Musial, and Hank Aaron as the lone major leaguers to play in 3,000 games. The 18-time All-Star and winner of the 1967 American League Triple Crown would retire after the 1983 season after spending all 23 of his big-league seasons with Boston. On May 25, Yastrzemski played first base and hit third in the lineup against, of all people, Len Barker. The game was a thriller. Cleveland raced to a 4-0 lead through four innings, but Yastrzemski played his part in the comeback, walking and scoring in a two-run Boston sixth inning. He also came through with a two-run single in the seventh, with the hosts eventually tying the game at six. With the two sides locked in a 7-7 deadlock entering the bottom of the ninth, Yaz led off with a walk. Following a double by Jim Rice and an intentional walk to Garry Hancock, Yastrzemski scored the game-winning run on Carney Lansford's single.

In both the American League and the National League, 1981 was becoming a banner season for MLB. Total attendance was 1.2 million ahead of 1980. Stadiums were filled to capacity as never before. Los Angeles was gripped by Fernandomania. Billy Martin reinvigorated the Oakland A's with "Billy Ball." Fans at Philadelphia's Veterans Stadium and other National League parks were mesmerized by Pete Rose, who was on the verge of passing Stan Musial as the National League's record hits leader in his quest to be the all-time "Hit King."

Given the gravity of Bench's injury, some might have predicted an immediate tailspin for Cincinnati. As it turns out, the seemingly irreplaceable legend was not needed, at least not in the short-term.

Cincinnati went 8-1 with a plus-19 run differential to start the month of June. Aside from Mike LaCoss serving up eight runs in a 15-7 bludgeoning by San Francisco on June 2, the Reds were untouchable. On June 11, the Reds bested the Mets 5-2. Facing his former team, Seaver struck out seven and walked one in a complete-game effort. A three-run bomb by George Foster broke a 2-2 deadlock in the sixth inning. To this point in the season, the Reds had a range of individual standouts.

On the pitching side, Seaver had compiled a 2.06 ERA in 12 starts, despite striking out only 52 batters in 87.1 innings. Mario Soto had been a true iron man, racking up at least seven innings in 11 of his 13 starts with six complete games. His final outing was his best, a 2-0 shutout of the host Mets. Soto fanned 12 and limited the Mets to six singles in a contest that lasted all of 134 minutes.

Offensively, the Big Red Machine's old workhorses remained productive. Concepción notched an impressive .807 OPS (on-base plus slugging percentage) and was an All-Star for the sixth consecutive year. Foster was named an All-Star for the fifth and final time after he launched 14 home runs and drove in 49 runs. The always-steady Ken Griffey, a Red since 1973, was hitting .300 before the All-Star break and patrolled center field with aplomb. He wound up with just two errors all season in 267 defensive chances.

NL WEST STANDINGS THROUGH JUNE 11

Team	Wins	Losses	Ties	W/L %	Games Back
Los Angeles Dodgers	36	21	0	.632	—
Cincinnati Reds	35	21	0	.625	0.5
Houston Astros	28	29	0	.491	8.0
Atlanta Braves	25	29	1	.463	9.5
San Francisco Giants	27	32	0	.458	10.0
San Diego Padres	23	33	0	.411	12.5

NL EAST STANDINGS THROUGH JUNE 11

Team	Wins	Losses	Ties	W/L %	Games Back
Philadelphia Phillies	34	21	0	.618	—
St. Louis Cardinals	30	20	1	.600	1.5
Montreal Expos	30	25	0	.545	4.0
Pittsburgh Pirates	25	23	1	.521	5.5
New York Mets	17	34	1	.333	15.0
Chicago Cubs	15	37	2	.288	17.5

AL WEST STANDINGS THROUGH JUNE 11

Team	Wins	Losses	Ties	W/L %	Games Back
Oakland Athletics	37	23	0	.617	—
Texas Rangers	33	22	0	.600	1.5
Chicago White Sox	31	22	0	.585	2.5
California Angels	31	29	0	.517	6.0
Kansas City Royals	20	30	0	.400	12.0
Seattle Mariners	21	36	1	.368	14.5
Minnesota Twins	17	39	1	.304	18.0

AL EAST STANDINGS THROUGH JUNE 11

Team	Wins	Losses	Ties	W/L %	Games Back
New York Yankees	34	22	0	.607	—
Baltimore Orioles	31	23	0	.574	2.0
Milwaukee Brewers	31	25	0	.554	3.0
Detroit Tigers	31	26	0	.544	3.5
Boston Red Sox	30	26	0	.536	4.0
Cleveland Indians	26	24	0	.520	5.0
Toronto Blue Jays	16	42	0	.276	19.0

"The owners are a group of men whose stupidity is exceeded by their avarice."

JONATHAN YARDLEY
LITERARY CRITIC AND SELF-PROCLAIMED BASEBALL FAN

9
The Trial Begins

9 A.M., OCTOBER 5

Major League Baseball was represented by five lawyers, with six paralegals squeezed behind their two oak tables on the left side of the courtroom. MLB's attorneys were buttoned up, looking smug, armed with one thin binder apiece. Seated beside the lawyers was Kuhn, one of the most hated sports commissioners in at least two big-league cities, St. Louis and Cincinnati. Kuhn joked with reporters beforehand about how frivolous all this was and that he had a plane waiting at the airport to go to Montreal for the first playoff game between the Dodgers and the Expos the next day. He chortled, "The engine is running. We won't be here long."

Wright, Chase, and DeMarco sat at one of the oak tables on the right side of the courtroom. They had the 24 boxes of documents stacked on the floor behind the table. Queen, Smack, Far, and the paralegals sat in the first row behind Wright and his colleagues. The lawyers seemed comfortable at the counsel table. The boys were sweating profusely. Queen looked around the courtroom and was in awe. "Jesus, I've never seen a courtroom like this, even on TV." Indeed, the room seemed to fit the importance of the occasion, with ceilings 35 feet high and three oak-paneled walls displaying oil portraits of 12 federal judges who had served on the bench before Chief Judge Jackson. A gray October sky was visible through the curtains on the outer wall.

Marvin Miller, the leader of what had become the most powerful union in America, sat in the back right corner, hardly noticed by the fans seated beside him. Ray Grebey, MLB's lead negotiator hired to battle Miller, sat in the left corner. He too was unnoticed by the crowd around him. Judge Jackson knew of both of them, as he had read newspaper accounts about their central roles in baseball's labor relations.

The courtroom bailiff, Archibald Graham, entered the room, followed by the judge. Graham was a retired physician, but he had played briefly in the majors 40 years earlier. (Briefly is an understatement; he played one inning in the outfield and hit one sacrifice fly.) Already seated at a table off to the side were three of the judge's law clerks: Josephine Wood, Del Ott, and Gillian Hodges. The clerks were exhausted, informing Graham they had burned the midnight oil studying the flurry of papers filed over the weekend by the plaintiffs and MLB.

Mr. Graham banged a gavel and announced "Hear ye, hear ye, this honorable court for the Southern District of Ohio is now in session. All persons having business before the court, draw attention, and ye shall be heard. God save the United States and this honorable court." The lawyers stood stiffly. Mr. Graham announced, "The first case on the docket this morning is Far, et al., versus Major League Baseball, et al., Case No. 1-CV-10-0006, the Honorable Joseph Jackson presiding."

Judge Jackson was not known for intellectual rigor. He often told colleagues that he reached decisions "as justice requires to advance the law." This reputation worried the MLB lawyers because they thought there was no existing case law or other legal precedent to support the plaintiffs' request for an injunction. MLB had filed a motion to dismiss the whole case the day before. The handsomely paid, experienced defense lawyers worried that Judge Jackson would "create" law and make them defend their unpopular position. Nonetheless, they already had their excuses ready for the owners if things went badly.

Jackson had a tremendous sense of humor, and, unlike most federal judges who avoided the spotlight, he was a social animal. He often had cocktails with attorneys who regularly appeared before him. He liked to get to the right decision, whether it took him weeks, months, or years. Jackson's keen interest in baseball and its revered history made Wright hopeful that the evidence would be fairly received.

Jackson got down to business. He had spent the early morning hours reading summaries of the case written by his law clerks. "Good morning. Welcome. I appreciate the parties and their counsel coming on such short notice and providing the court with their respective positions. I do not believe any of the counsel from out of state have appeared before me, and I look forward to working with you. Mr. Dowd, you may proceed, since it is your motion we have to deal with first."

MLB's lead lawyer, John Dowd, rose to his feet. In a manner befitting a corporate lawyer, he sported a tailored Brooks Brothers suit and a bright red tie. He pointedly asked the judge to dispense with the lawsuit and allow baseball to get back to business. After summarizing the history of the labor dispute for what seemed to the boys to be an eternity and calling Kuhn's decision to split the season "Solomon-like," he concluded: "Your Honor, as we laid out for the court yesterday, a request like this is unprecedented in the history of this country's jurisprudence. There is no legal authority for halting a private sports organization from holding any sort of competition like the one at hand. Delaying the playoffs will cause irreparable damage to baseball and its television partners, not to mention its fans. What's more, time is of the essence as we approach the first scheduled game." He then returned to his seat next to Kuhn, who nudged him approvingly.

Dowd decided not to address the central factual issue in the case: the unprecedented denial of the teams with the best records from participating in the playoffs. He left the door open for Wright to set the record straight.

A federal mediator is called to the rescue.

10

Storm Clouds Lead to Thunder

MAY 1981

On the labor front, sports and business pages around the country detailed the bad news as May drew to a close: MLB owners and the union remained at loggerheads. The May 29 strike date that had been targeted by the union was fast approaching. The free agent compensation committee assembled in 1980 to avert a strike that year had come up short in 1981: eight meetings, no progress. A federal mediator, Ken Moffett, was called in to help broker a solution. Moffett, the son of a union man, was acting director of the Federal Mediation and Conciliation Service. He had spent the last two decades successfully mediating and settling strikes. Moffett's secret: he was witty, gregarious, charming, and disarming with an Alfred E. Neuman "What, me worry?" style. Surely, he could bring the two sides together.

Moffett had his hands full in 1981. He was charged with the task of helping the Federal Aviation Administration and the Professional Air Traffic Controllers Organization (PATCO) reach agreement on a new contract while simultaneously working with the baseball owners and players. These were high-profile battles, and Moffett was not your typical mediator. He made the rounds to talk shows to talk about the progress of negotiations, or lack thereof, because he enjoyed the spotlight. Even *Playboy* magazine was asking for an interview. "It's really been crazy. I went to Baltimore yesterday and I was having a slice of pizza and a couple of kids came up for an autograph and there's this guy taking pictures with this zoom lens, about 30 feet away. I've certainly had my share of recognition, with the longshoreman's strike, the 1978 New York newspaper strike. But this is crazy."

As is the case with most labor disputes, both PATCO and the players' union were seeking to protect their members' financial interests. The 13,000 federal air traffic controllers were demanding a salary increase of $10,000 annually, while the players were trying to protect their ever-inflating salaries, some of which grew by hundreds of thousands of dollars in one season. Moffett shuttled between bargaining sessions for the two disputes. He was frustrated with both and told *The Washington Post* that the air traffic controllers "whoop, they holler, and they believe their situation is comparable to a pro athlete. They're prima donnas. Egoists."

When PATCO told him, "We're gonna win big or lose big," he told them "that's bullshit," adding, "you are like lemmings running into the sea." He warned them they were underestimating the government's resolve.

On the baseball front, it appeared the teams were blustering as well. Bob Howsam of the Reds warned the owners, "Gentlemen, let me tell you something. This is your only chance to achieve something. If you capitulate this time, you'll never achieve anything again. It's now or never." In contrast with Moffett's small, closed-door negotiations with PATCO, he faced a unique challenge with the baseball dispute: not only did Miller and his lieutenants attend the mediation sessions as would be customary, they were typically accompanied by dozens of ballplayers who wanted to be heard. Grebey complained that there were "sometimes 30, 40, 50 guys!"

When opposing sides in a dispute are intransigent and have no desire to compromise, there is little that even a skilled negotiator like Moffett can do. The MLB dispute was unique in that it was a one-issue negotiation (free agency compensation) with no chips to swap. As his efforts to extract a compromise continued toward the May 29 strike date, he realized no deal would be consummated. What he did not know was that Miller wanted to avert a strike.

The owners consistently spoke publicly about the economic hardships facing the sport, echoing Kuhn's claim that "the prospect of staggering losses for our clubs is an emphatically real prospect." Bob Lurie, owner of the San Francisco Giants, forewarned a disaster: "Just wait until one or two teams go under."

Miller was frustrated; the owners were careful not to claim economic hardship at the negotiating table because that would force them to open their books. Nonetheless, the union chief thought the public statements before and after private negotiating sessions should be enough under the law to force the owners to open their books. And so the union then turned to its sole legal option to avert a strike: Miller filed an unfair labor practice charge with the National Labor Relations Board (NLRB), claiming that the owners were not negotiating in good faith by refusing to provide data about their finances. If the NLRB agreed, such a ruling could have a major impact on the situation, avert the May 29 strike, and possibly break the logjam.

Just 24 hours before the strike deadline, the NLRB decided to support the union's claim by issuing a complaint against the owners that required the owners to provide the financial data requested by Miller. The NLRB also paused implementation of the owners' free agent compensation plan for up to one year. The owners immediately appealed to federal court. Play continued and Moffett's hair continued to turn gray. Miller was hopeful the tactic would compel the owners to blink.

> "We are here today because of sheer hypocrisy motivated by financial greed, something baseball has never tolerated."
>
> **GEORGE WRIGHT**

11

The Plaintiffs Educate the Judge

LATE MORNING, OCTOBER 5

"Very well then," Jackson bellowed. "Mr. Wright, let's hear from the fans." Wright's colleague, DeMarco, had prepared Wright's response to the motion to dismiss the evening before. The gray-haired lawyer looked like a classic trial lawyer—a Perry Mason type—who commanded attention just by the way he carried himself. Wright grabbed his leather briefcase that was jammed with his handwritten notes, walked to the lectern, and began. "May it please the court. Let me tell you the undisputed background to our story that brought us here. That will allow us to get to the point with each witness."

Jackson interjected: "I have read the pleadings, Mr. Wright, so brevity would be appreciated. We are approaching the noon hour."

Wright began:

> Thank you, Judge Jackson. We are here today because of sheer hypocrisy motivated by financial greed, something baseball has never tolerated. Baseball has always prided itself on the integrity of the game. The Cincinnati Reds and the St. Louis Cardinals should be in this year's postseason. The Reds had the best record in the

National League, and indeed all of baseball, and the Cardinals won their division. But MLB was afraid that the strike had driven fans away from the sport, so they came up with a split-season concept to keep more fans interested in baseball when play resumed. Instead of having just two teams in each league contend for the league title, MLB devised a shortsighted plan to keep supporters of eight MLB teams interested. And not surprisingly—in light of MLB's obsession with the bottom line—the team with the biggest fan base, the New York Yankees, was one that unfairly landed a playoff spot under the split-season arrangement. This ploy was cleverly designed to increase MLB's profits from ticket sales and TV revenue since there would be more postseason games to be televised. The higher the number of games, the more advertising spots could be sold. It backfired because the public recognized it as a sham.

The three law students, no longer perspiring, smiled as Wright set up the products of two long nights' work: eight 6-foot x 10-foot foam boards that displayed the timeline outlined in his presentation. By appearance, the boards were somewhat amateurish, as they lacked both color and fancy graphics. Still they enabled the judge to see the story visually. After all, the students had learned in their trial practice class that judges and juries grasp lawyers' contentions best when they can see them as well as hear them. Wright spoke eloquently and in a relaxed manner. Knowing Jackson was a sports fan, he summarized the labor dispute, introduced the key players, and then talked about the split season. Wright understood that the audience in the courtroom behind him did not need to hear the narrative because they had all lived through it as financial stakeholders or rabid fans, but his real audience, Jackson, hardly knew the intricacies of the season and the strike.

Then he wrapped up his remarks: "After their miscalculation about the players' willingness to strike in 1980, the owners again misjudged the union's resolve in 1981. This error led directly to the betrayal of the fans' century-long trust after a third of the 1981 season had already transpired, and during what had the look of one of the most exciting seasons of all-time. We plan to prove the illegality of all this through four witnesses: Jim Far, a baseball historian; Bowie Kuhn; Marvin Miller; and Ray Grebey. Thank you." Far rather liked his new moniker of "historian."

Wright turned, glanced at the boys, and winked. He thought he had gotten the judge's attention, and they had to agree. They were pleased with their lawyer. It was now almost 1:00 p.m., and the courtroom was eerily silent. Would Judge Jackson grant MLB's motion to dismiss?

Jackson broke the silence. "Thank you, gentlemen. This matter was well-briefed on short notice, and I appreciate the background you have provided this morning. I will consider the matter over the lunch hour, and then the court will resume at 2:30 p.m. I need time to digest my sandwich and your arguments about this pressing matter."

At that, the clerk banged the gavel. "This honorable court is adjourned until 2:30 p.m."

A thrilling season is halted.

12
Strike Three

KEN MOFFETT COULD NOT FIND A SOLUTION. Judge Henry Frederick Werker summoned the union and owners to the United States District Court for the Southern District of New York to adjudicate the owners' appeal of the NLRB's order that temporarily stopped the strike. The union came armed with press clippings of the gloom and doom statements from the owners and tried to throw them in the owners' faces. The owners responded by saying that they had never made an issue of their economic condition during negotiations. After two days of hearings, Judge Werker overruled the NLRB. He found the union's claim that the owners needed to turn over financial data was a "bargaining tactic by the Association to prevent the implementation of the [owners'] proposal." Judge Werker concluded his order with "PLAY BALL!!! SO ORDERED." Werker's order to continue play was short-lived. The players had up to 48 hours to decide whether to strike after Werker's decision.

Against the backdrop of failed negotiations over the winter and players' insistence that direct compensation for a free agent would never happen, the 1981 season so far was one of the most riveting in history. The four divisional leaders on June 11—Los Angeles and Philadelphia in the National League, and New York and Oakland in the American League—were in first place by no more than two games. It was only the second time that all four divisional races had been that competitive that far into the season since divisional play began in 1969. What a season to look forward to when the players and owners came to their senses!

In the NL West, the Reds (35-21) sat just a half-game back of the Dodgers (36-21). The Reds not only owned the second-best winning percentage in the division (.625), but also in all of Major League Baseball. Reds fans had enjoyed the rivalry with the Dodgers over the last decade, and it appeared the pennant race would be a doozy. Pete Rose's Phillies led the NL East (34-21), at least partly by virtue of having played six more games than the second-place St. Louis Cardinals (30-20). Oakland owned the American League's top spot (37-23) and was a game and a half ahead of the Texas Rangers (33-22) in the AL West. The Yankees (34-22) were two games ahead of Baltimore (31-23) in the East, and four other squads were also within five games of first place.

The union and the owners met on June 11, with the former suddenly giving an inch. Miller proposed that a compensation pool of major league players be used as compensation to a team losing a free agent. A large number of players attended the negotiation session, including high-priced veterans George Foster, Joe Niekro, and Don Sutton. Grebey thought it was a tactic designed by Miller to play to the crowd, especially with stars showing support for the union. At the end of the meeting, Miller announced, "I gather from [Grebey's] comments that they don't like our proposal . . . strike begins tomorrow."

As Rose approached Stan Musial's National League record of 3,630 hits, the Phillies had arranged for 3,631 balloons to be released if Rose tallied two hits that evening.

Rose, a switch-hitter by age eight, was a product of Western Hills High School in Cincinnati. His trademark competitiveness was ingrained in him by his father, Harry. Although a star athlete, Rose did not make academics a priority (he was forced to repeat the ninth grade). Because he had used all four years of his eligibility by the end of his junior season, he was ineligible to play for Western Hills' high school team during his senior year. Rose played semipro ball instead. Luckily for Rose, his uncle, Buddy Bloebaum, was a scout for the Reds and made it a priority for Rose to sign with his hometown club. Rose signed with the Reds the day he graduated from Western Hills in 1960, and he immediately started in the Reds farm system.

After tearing up the minors for three years, Rose debuted in the majors in 1963 and won Rookie of the Year, playing second base for a squad that had Frank Robinson and Vada Pinson in the outfield and Jim Maloney, Jim O'Toole, and Joe Nuxhall in the starting rotation. Rose arrived as the Reds were stuck between eras: they had reached the World Series in 1961, but they were still years away from developing players and making trades (both good and bad) that would form the basis of the Big Red Machine. During Rose's first seven seasons with the Reds, the club never captured the NL pennant, but they finished below .500 only once.

Rose thrived even when the Reds were not at their peak, earning All-Star nods while playing multiple positions. He was an All-Star in 1965 at second base; again in 1967 stationed primarily in left field; and from 1968-69 after a move to right field, leading the majors in hitting both seasons. Rose garnered his lone MVP award in 1973, racking up an 8.3-WAR season and his third batting title, along with 230 hits. After making the All-Star team from

1967 through 1971, he was not chosen in 1972. In 1973, Rose began a streak of 10 consecutive All-Star seasons. During the Big Red Machine's back-to-back championships in 1975 and 1976, Rose led the majors in games played, runs, and doubles, and he finished in the top five of the NL MVP voting in both seasons. In 1975, he once again changed positions for the betterment of the team, moving to third base from the outfield to ensure Foster's powerful bat could become an everyday presence in the lineup. Rose was MVP of the 1975 World Series, hitting .370 and reaching base 16 times in 33 plate appearances.

In 1976, Rose led the majors in hits (215) for the sixth time in a 7.0-WAR season. During the postseason, he hit .429 in the NLCS versus Philadelphia, but just .188 in 19 plate appearances against the Yankees in the World Series. Rose remained productive in his final two seasons with Cincinnati, hitting .311 in 1977 and .302 in 1978. Rose's final four All-Star appearances came with the Phillies from 1979 to 1982. In 1983, he was reunited with Perez and Morgan on the Phillies. That year, the Phillies advanced all the way to the World Series, Rose's sixth Fall Classic. He hit .313 as Philadelphia lost to Baltimore in five games. Rose returned to the Reds in 1984 as player-manager, and on September 11, 1985, he broke Ty Cobb's all-time hits record. Rose played his last season at age 45 in 1986 and then managed Cincinnati into the 1989 season. His jersey number, 14, was retired by the Reds in 2016. Rose died at age 83 in September 2024.

A capacity crowd turned out to see Rose equal the record against future Hall of Fame pitcher Nolan Ryan. Rose, now the Philadelphia Phillies' quadragenarian first baseman, singled in his first at-bat versus Ryan—

another baseball legend who would play well into his 40s—for career hit No. 3,630, his only hit of the night. Rose had equaled Musial's mark, and the crowd gave him a prolonged standing ovation. "When I got that first hit I felt 20," said Rose postgame, "and when I struck out the next three times I felt 40."

The celebratory balloons went flat shortly thereafter—along with the season—as the players went on strike the next day. Unbeknownst to the fans, players, and owners, the first 11 days of June 1981 had constituted a playoff race. They would find out in September just how critical those prestrike games were, along with the disparity in games played, in deciding the postseason competition.

> "Once upon a time, baseball was the national pastime. Now that status is being challenged by the NFL. This current debacle only helps football."

JIM FAR
BASEBALL FAN

13

Jim Far Becomes a Star

AFTERNOON, OCTOBER 5

WRIGHT, HIS COLLEAGUES, AND THE BOYS headed to the nearby Clock Restaurant to grab a quick lunch. Far asked Wright how he thought Jackson was leaning. "I think he's paying attention. We should win the motion to dismiss, and I think he will give us a chance. It's difficult to dismiss a case like this with so much national attention. I expect he will ask questions as we go along. I was somewhat surprised he didn't interrupt us."

Wright continued, "We have a garden to grow, and Marvin Miller will plant the seeds. Whoever said he should be the first witness after Jim tells the fans' story was right." Wright winked at Smack; it was his idea, however obvious it might have been. "If we can get him on the stand, he should help us, although you never know. We don't even know if he approved the split season. Someone should scour the research and find that out before he testifies tomorrow."

Smack jumped at the opportunity. "I'll run back there now and begin looking through the boxes."

Back at the courthouse, Kuhn, Dowd, and the other MLB attorneys met privately in an anteroom. The room typically housed witnesses waiting to appear, but it was available for informal conferences by trial lawyers as long as they didn't displace any witnesses. The six men chomped on sandwiches delivered by a local bagel store. Kuhn looked at Dowd: "Jack, I thought I would be out of here by 10:00. What's going on? Your team was so confident."

Dowd was direct in his response: "Bowie, you know these things are never slam dunks. Sure, I thought we would get the case dismissed, but the judge has a lot of public pressure on him. He has to find a way to reach the right decision without looking like he is on our side. We'll be alright."

Kuhn was now worried about tomorrow's scheduled Divisional Playoff game. "Do you think we will be outta here by 3:00?"

Dowd shrugged his shoulders. "Who knows? If he doesn't toss this bullshit—and I'd say it's a 60-40 chance that he will—you better plan to stay through Wednesday. You may have to move the games to Friday, but that's the worst case."

"Jesus Christ. 60–40? That's a lot less than you said yesterday," Kuhn said. "We can't move the games. It will cost millions."

"Tell that to the judge and you'll guarantee we lose not only the motion but the whole damn thing," Dowd said. "You heard Wright, he's painting the owners as greedy bastards. We all know a few days won't matter. Even if we play the Series in early November, fans don't mind cold, fall games."

With all the parties back in their places, Judge Jackson entered the overflowing courtroom at precisely 2:30 p.m.

"Let me start the afternoon by announcing I have decided to deny the motion to dismiss filed last evening by the defendants. I believe that there are significant issues involved here, which require a more thorough legal analysis than suggested by the defendants."

Jackson continued: "I am halting the playoffs until the court can make a reasoned decision on the legal issues, but I understand the urgency. There is a legitimate issue about whether the defendants cheated the fans, but I have not made up my mind. I am prepared to hear the matter on the merits now, if both parties are prepared. Mr. Wright, as counsel for the plaintiffs, are you so prepared?"

A cheer went up from the rows of fans. The rapping of the gavel reverberated off the walls. "I will not tolerate any outbursts in this courtroom," bellowed Jackson.

George Grande rushed out of the packed courtroom, and ESPN broke into a tape-delayed broadcast of a wrestling match to report the announcement. Scrolling along the bottom of the screen was this chyron: BREAKING NEWS: FEDERAL JUDGE IN COLUMBUS, OHIO, SAYS TRIAL WILL PROCEED TO HALT MLB PLAYOFFS. Grande summarized the goings-on in the courtroom and concluded his 10-minute interruption with, "More on SportsCenter tonight. Now, back to wrestling!"

CNN broke into its entertainment coverage of the TV debut of *The Smurfs* with a live report from David Walker live outside the courthouse on Marconi Boulevard. "I hate to interrupt the discussion of the tiny blue creatures that live in a peaceful forest, but I have news about the Dodgers and other MLB teams in a war with some of their fans. I don't believe this folks, but it looks like the fans' challenge to the baseball playoffs may not be a joke after all. We will have extensive coverage on CNN Newsroom tonight at 5:00!"

Back in the courtroom, Wright aimed to seize the momentum Judge Jackson had afforded him. "I am so prepared, Your Honor. It will take several hours to present our evidence." Jackson knew most trial lawyers underestimate the time they need to make their case, but he nodded as if he agreed.

"Do you also have witnesses to call?" asked Jackson.

"Yes, Your Honor. We plan to call one of our clients, Mr. Far, as well as Marvin Miller and Ray Grebey," Wright replied.

Jackson turned to the stunned lawyers seated to his right. "Is the defense so prepared?"

Dowd stood. "May we be heard further?"

Jackson replied curtly. "No. There is always a first case under any legal theory. Are you prepared to try the case on the merits, or would you like a delay?"

"Your Honor, we had no notice that witnesses would be called, so we object to having Mr. Grebey testify," Dowd said.

"Why is that? Jackson asked, with a tone of disbelief. "He was introduced earlier and is here. What possible prejudice to your clients would result if he testifies?"

"It's just that we should be able to prepare a defense," said Dowd, stumbling over his words. "We had no notice of the witnesses being called."

"Well, would you like some time to better prepare?" offered Jackson.

Dowd turned to Kuhn, who no longer appeared confident and relaxed. Kuhn shook his head in response. Dowd informed the judge: "No, Your Honor. The playoffs start tomorrow and there is too much at stake."

Jackson turned to Wright. "Call your first witness."

"James Far," interjected Wright, almost before the judge had finished speaking.

The law student knew he was going to be the first witness, but he was startled nonetheless. He had never been a witness before. He was studying to become a lawyer so he could be the one asking the questions, not answering them. He stood, straightened his green tie, and proceeded to the chair in his khaki pants, white button-down shirt, and blue sport coat.

Jackson looked at Wright. "I approve of hearing from one of the plaintiffs, but I anticipate this testimony will not take as long as that of the other witnesses. Agreed?"

"Of course," said Wright, gaining confidence by the minute.

With the judge's admonition in mind, Wright asked Far to provide a brief background about himself. Far was a Detroit Tigers fan who grew up in Toledo, Ohio, just across the border from Michigan. He referred to himself as a baseball purist, enjoying the Tigers in his youth when they won the 1968 World Series, but he explained that he loved the game more than he loved his team.

Far had been a history major at Notre Dame and loved exploring the past. He turned and faced the judge, as Wright had advised him to do, and explained to Jackson that he considered himself a baseball historian. "One day, I'd like to work in Major League Baseball, but something tells me that is not going to happen," he said with a wry smile. "Maybe I'll be a player's agent and work with Mr. Miller."

Wright interrupted. "Tell the court why you and your colleagues filed this suit." Far laughed to himself because he thought no one had ever called his friends "colleagues." But he replied directly, as rehearsed over lunch. Far began,

> Your Honor, long before I became a fan, baseball was the national pastime. Now that status is being challenged by the NFL. This current debacle only helps football. From 1903 through 1968, a group of teams in the National League and another group in the American League, under the auspices of Major League Baseball, would begin play in April each year. In September, the two teams with the most wins in each league would face each other in the World Series. Of

course, calling it the World Series was a bit of an exaggeration since the championship was limited to teams from North America, but baseball fans did not care about that. It was a tradition based upon a well-understood and time-tested principle: only the two teams with the best season-long record could compete for the championship. The purpose behind the World Series, of course, was to crown a champion that fans could recognize as the best team in baseball. Not incidentally, the Series has evolved into a major moneymaker for MLB.

Besides hosting a championship series, another hallowed tradition in baseball has involved maintaining the integrity of the game. Baseball has always condemned cheating and, in particular, cheating for financial gain. In 1919, MLB accused eight players from the Chicago White Sox of throwing the World Series, ironically, to the Cincinnati Reds. The charge was that the White Sox players were paid money in exchange for intentionally losing games. For their transgression, the eight White Sox players who were implicated were labeled the Black Sox. The commissioner came down hard on the alleged cheaters and tossed them out of the game permanently. Baseball has treated cheating with unqualified opprobrium ever since that scandal. We believe Major League Baseball has violated the integrity of the game by cheating fans out of a fair playoff system this year.

In 1969, MLB decided to create two divisions within both the National League and the American League, each with an equal number of teams. This meant that the division winners in each league had to face each other in a best-of-five series to determine who would advance to the World Series. Season-ticket holders from every team had the right to purchase World Series tickets if their team made it that far.

I have to digress here a little and talk about the players and their union. In the beginning—and for almost the entire first century of professional baseball's existence—the owners controlled basically everything. In the first decade or two of professional baseball, from 1869 to about 1880, players freely shopped their services around and made pretty decent money for the day, but in the 1880s the owners imposed the infamous reserve clause, making it part of every player's contract. The reserve clause gave teams the rights to a player's services in perpetuity, disallowing players' control over their professional lives. Owners offered players one-year contracts at a wage they determined, and they retained the option to keep or trade players at their discretion. Their attitude was that if players didn't like it, they could move on and take a job in some other industry.

Not that the players completely laid down in response. They mounted a few efforts at unionizing over the years. Indeed, in 1890 they even started their own competing league. That league lasted exactly one season and, for the next half century, little came of the players' efforts.

In the 1940s, in response to some additional but ultimately aborted efforts by players to unionize, the owners set up a pension system. Pensions were, primarily, what the players had been seeking, so this concession assuaged them for a while. By the late 1940s, it became clear that the pension plan was woefully underfunded, so in 1953 the players formed the Major League Baseball Players Association. All-Star pitcher Bob Feller was its first president. The Association, as Feller preferred to call it, was advised by a labor lawyer named J. Norman Lewis. Lewis personally opposed the notion of striking and

> supported the reserve system. He worked for the same law firm that represented the New York Giants owners, which raised questions over a conflict of interest. The early union had no office, and since players weren't big fans of paying dues, the mostly powerless Association was mostly insolvent as well.
>
> The union, nonetheless, carried on for the next decade, with Lewis eventually being fired and Feller stepping down in 1959. The next leader, Judge Robert Cannon, was only a part-time legal advisor. Worse, he was even more conflicted than Lewis in that he wanted to be the baseball commissioner and openly lobbied for the job. To the extent that this troubled the players, it was counterbalanced by their unwillingness to own the idea of a strong union. The players—thanks to an extraordinarily successful, century-long, owner-led propaganda campaign that convinced them they were privileged to play a game for a living—were wary of hiring a straightforward labor advocate to lead the union. In addition, they were up against some societal anti-union sentiment at the time, tying unions with the mob, corruption, and ugly strikes. The players wanted secure paychecks, but they didn't want to be part of perceived wrongdoing.
>
> It was not until they hired a pro in Marvin Miller that things changed, and I understand Mr. Miller will talk about that. All he did was attempt to balance the scales since they had been tilted in the owners' favor for so long.

Far shifted in his chair and drew a deep breath:

> Back to the playoffs. The 1969 change that watered down the World Series was bad enough. But what Major League Baseball did this summer was a betrayal of its promises to ticket-buying fans that only the best teams over the entire course of a season would play for the championship. That is why millions of people care about

the baseball season. If teams were just randomly selected for the postseason, why would anyone spend their time and energy attending, watching, listening to, or reading about the regular season? MLB never told the fans anything would be different until we endured the strike this summer, and then the owners schemed behind closed doors to recoup their losses. Talk about a lack of integrity!

Most importantly, they promised each team's season-ticket buyers that if their team qualified for the playoffs, they would be given the chance to buy playoff tickets. This promise has been part of season-ticket solicitations for decades, so it has been a major selling point for fans, particularly since World Series tickets arguably have been the hardest sports tickets to get in this country for much of this century.

Turning toward Judge Jackson, Far said,

Starting in 1946, my parents bought our family a 15-game season ticket packet every year for the next 30 years. Because they did that, in 1968 I attended a World Series game—an experience I will never forget. I don't think my dad would be a Tigers' season ticket holder without the promise of postseason tickets. Our Exhibit 2 contains copies of various MLB teams' season-ticket agreements.

Mr. Queen's parents decided to buy a Reds season ticket package last winter. Even though only Mr. Queen is a Reds fan, Mr. Smack and I wanted to go to games this season, and we used Queen's parents' tickets several times. The Tigers weren't likely to win this year, but we believed this may be the last year that the remaining Big Red Machine members would compete for a World Series title, and we wanted to be there.

We filed this lawsuit because the Reds earned the right to take part in the playoffs, fair and square. As such, we and thousands of other fans should be in Riverfront Stadium tomorrow watching them play instead of sitting in this courtroom. I hope we can still have the chance to see them play in the World Series.

Wright beamed with pride. "Thank you, Mr. Far. No more questions."

Dowd had no idea if he should ask any questions. Far's history lesson was accurate, by and large, but it was hard to ignore the urge to ask *something*. Dowd decided to fish for something sinister, though he had not come prepared with any bait. "Mr. Far, did anyone from the union or any of the players ask you and your friends to file this lawsuit?"

"Not at all," Far said. "We did not even contact Mr. Wright until Saturday, and we've never met or spoken to Mr. Miller. We wrote several letters to Mr. Kuhn this summer, but he never responded."

Dowd didn't want to dig any deeper of a hole than he was already in. "No further questions."

It was now after 5:00 p.m., so Judge Jackson adjourned the court until the next morning.

Meanwhile, the media coverage was exploding. Grande broke into a televised volleyball match to sum up Far's testimony. "If today was a baseball game, the fans scored several runs early in the game. The owners tried to keep the game simple, but there's no question the umpire is not sure of the call to make. We will hear from Marvin Miller tomorrow. That should be interesting!"

NBC and ABC announced on the evening news that the playoff games scheduled for the next day were "indefinitely suspended. Mr. Far presented convincing testimony about the folly of the split season."

"Gavel," the world's largest steel sculpture, serves as the centerpiece of the reflecting pool between the two justice buildings in downtown Columbus, Ohio.

The split season is born.

14
A Long Two Months

BASEBALL FANS ASSUMED THAT the players and owners were trying their best to end the strike. To determine whose side most fans were on, the commissioner and team owners took a close look at the polls. An NBC survey found that 53 percent of fans sided with the owners; other measures of public opinion were even more lopsided in favor of the owners. Polls by the *New York Daily News* and the *Cleveland Plain Dealer* revealed that two-thirds of baseball fans believed players had no right to complain. Players' average pay of $196,000 for playing a game drew little sympathy, especially from the legions of college baseball players and minor leaguers who would have loved to take their place.

Many fans found solace during the strike by attending minor league games. Newspaper sports sections scrambled to fill the void by running game stories from previous seasons or reporting on fictional games as the strike continued. For example, one writer from the *Philadelphia Inquirer* wrote about his dream that Pete Rose had finally broken Musial's hits record. TV stations rebroadcast classic games.

Commissioner Kuhn was caught in a pickle. Fans thought he should make good on his claim that he would not take either side. They wanted him to find a way to resolve the dispute and get players back on the field. On the other hand, some owners informed Kuhn that he had dropped the ball. Edward Bennett Williams, the owner of the Baltimore Orioles, met with Kuhn on June 16 and told him bluntly, "This is the end of our friendship."

Eddie Chiles, owner of the Texas Rangers, attacked Kuhn the next day: "You are sitting here in your fancy office doing nothing. If you can't figure out anything else to do, you could at least put your desk out on the sidewalk and talk to fans. It is up to you to do something! But as far as I can see, you are not doing a damned thing. I won't tolerate that! You and Lee MacPhail work for me! I pay your salaries! You are just like any other employees I have got. I tell you what to do, and you are supposed to do it."

Kuhn, in response, called Chiles a lamebrained old fool, adding, "I find your remarks nothing short of insulting, and as far as I'm concerned, you can get the hell out of here!"

To everyone's surprise, Miller did not participate when the negotiations resumed on June 17. Some owners thought that Miller was extremely clever at tactical maneuvering, but he was not so good at the bargaining table. They believed he had little sense of timing and virtually no idea how to close a deal. This weakness was compounded by his visible hatred for Grebey and the owners.

As stunning as it was that Miller absented himself, his strategy had a specific purpose: the owners and Kuhn claimed that he had become the barrier to resolution and that reasonable players would compromise if only Miller stepped aside. So by backing away from the table, Miller called the owners' bluff. He turned the negotiations over to a players' committee consisting of well known players: Doug DeCinces, Bob Boone, Phil Garner, Steve Rogers, and Mark Belanger. They, like Miller, distrusted Grebey.

Rogers, a star pitcher for Montreal, accused Grebey of being "condescending to us and making us feel that we did not know anything ... When he laid out the figures for us, he made it seem that we couldn't understand any of it. We could handle some numbers." Rogers was angry and sarcastic. He had a degree in petroleum engineering, and he helped develop a computer program used by players in salary arbitration.

During one of the negotiation sessions, Boone went over to the management side and started imitating Grebey by saying, "Trust me. Trust me." Belanger took about three steps and dove, headfirst, right across the table, and slid right into Boone's lap.

Moffett recalled, "I have seen fistfights. I have broken up fistfights, but I've never seen anything like that." As negotiations continued without any progress, the players told Moffett that they no longer wanted to meet with the owners because it was "Chinese water torture." They suggested that Fernando Valenzuela attend instead. When Moffett told them Valenzuela did not speak English, the players retorted that he did. He could say "More beer!"

During the second week of the strike, the owners' Lloyd's of London insurance policy kicked in. Each club collected $100,000 per game once the first 161 games had been canceled. That amount would be paid for up to 500 lost games, which would cover any scheduled games until August 8. With that level of guaranteed income, the owners had far less financial incentive to resolve the strike than they had had when the strike first started.

With millions of dollars and the 1981 season on the line, the union filed a grievance on June 23 to remind the owners that they would be accountable for even the smallest infraction of the collective bargaining agreement. The grievance claimed that 12 players and one coach had to pay $27.50 for drinks on an early-season flight because they did not get first-class meals while seated in coach. While the union asserted that the owners were still obligated to handle everyday matters even in the midst of the strike, the owners thought the grievance was a testament to the absurdity of the players' greed.

Moffett tried his best to calm the players. He explained that Grebey was in a tough spot. He had owners and general managers who did not always agree, so in some ways they were less united than the players. In addition, the commissioner was largely absent from the negotiations. Moffett found support from one editorialist who opined that "if Bowie Kuhn was alive, this would never have happened."

Miller returned to the bargaining table in early July. But negotiations were still at a standstill. When Doug DeCinces was asked to pose for a picture in a T-shirt saying "I Survived the 1981 Baseball Strike," he declined. He was not sure he, or baseball, would survive. The players began to squabble among themselves as the strike continued. Dodgers second baseman Davey Lopes called the negotiations "a circus" and questioned the players' representatives: "I don't think they have credentials to be in a labor meeting. Do Doug DeCinces and Bob Boone have legal backgrounds? I don't see any postal clerks going into their negotiations."

Miller immediately arranged a meeting with the players in Chicago to defuse the tension. After a five and a half hour meeting with the 26 player representatives and about 30 others who lived in the area, Cubs pitcher Mike Krukow announced that all of his concerns had been satisfied by Miller. The rest of the attendees had also become true believers.

Next, Miller traveled to Los Angeles, which was Lopes country. About 45 players attended, including Lopes and other player representatives. After two and a half hours, Minnesota Twins star Rod Carew called for a voice vote. Seventy voices said "aye" in response to whether the strike should continue; there were no "nay" votes. Lopes approached DeCinces and said "I'm sorry for criticizing your role." The owners will blink, believed the players.

On July 14, the day of the scheduled All-Star game, 15,000 fans gathered in downtown Cleveland to express their displeasure over the game not being played. When the first pitch was supposed to have been delivered, they let loose a collective boo registering at 130 decibels. Milwaukee Brewers president Bud Selig was at lunch when a fan told him, "I agree with you guys, Bud."

Selig replied, "Well, thank you. I sure hope it all works out."

The fan tried to show his support in stronger terms: "I'll never pay a nickel to see those SOBs play again." *Great,* thought Selig, *where does that leave me?*

As the owners continued to squabble even more, the Orioles' owner, Edward Bennett Williams, interceded. He called Ray Donovan, the US secretary of labor, and asked him to join the talks. They already had Moffett as a mediator, but Donovan agreed to try and help. After all, baseball was the national pastime, and it was in the national interest to resolve the dispute.

After the owners realized the players remained united behind Miller, they grew weary of Grebey. They turned to Lee MacPhail, American League president, to cut a deal. The owners realized that they were losing, and they wanted to end the strike. On July 30, MacPhail waved the white flag and forged an agreement with the union that the owners thought they would never have to make. Twenty-four teams signed on, with the notable exception of the Cincinnati Reds and the St. Louis Cardinals. The new agreement awarded a team losing a free agent one player from a free agency compensation pool. Clubs who signed free agents could protect 24 players on their major league roster. Any clubs that didn't sign free agents could protect 26. When all was said and done, the union had prevailed on almost every issue. The new agreement enshrined free agency and even increased the minimum player salary. To add insult to injury, the players even got full-service credit for the games that were canceled because of the strike.

Miller hoped that some of the new guard in baseball recognized two essential truths: the union could not be broken, and long-term cooperation was the only way to ensure that future strikes would be averted. Johnny Bench of the Reds was particularly happy. "Marvin gave players freedom and money that has made the game better for everyone," he said. Bench was a longtime supporter of the union chief. In 1972, when the players went on their first successful strike from April 1 to 13, Bench was a vocal supporter of Miller. Bench received a cool reception from disapproving Reds fans on April 15 during Opening Day introductions after the strike had been resolved. Nonetheless, the fans had short memories and cheered for "JB" throughout his MVP season that year.

When it came time to announce the deal to the public, neither Grebey nor Miller was willing to shake hands with the other or pose in the traditional photograph commemorating the settlement. Asked about his relationship with federal mediator Ken Moffett, Grebey replied curtly, "No comment."

Gussie Busch of the Cardinals was angry. "I have never been more disgusted, angry, and ashamed of a situation in which I was involved. Once again, we are being ridiculed by everyone—inside and outside of sports."

On the other hand, Jerry Reinsdorf, owner of the Chicago White Sox, was happy. "I don't think there was any point, from the owners' standpoint, to this strike...There's a small minority of us who have been pushing...to get this settled. This is an instance where the majority doesn't know what's good for it."

Both sides in the baseball strike lost approximately $28 million, with owners more than making up the foregone revenue by taking in $44 million in strike insurance payouts for the 712 games that didn't happen. But in all the ways that mattered, it was Marvin Miller's finest hour. The union had been strengthened, not broken. In fact, some observers who were well versed in labor negotiations considered the Major League Baseball Players Association America's most successful union.

After two long months without major league baseball, play was scheduled to resume on August 9 with the All-Star Game. Regular-season games were to start back up the next day. But the question remained about how to handle the end-of-season playoffs given the long interruption in play. Commissioner Kuhn, well aware of his diminishing support among MLB owners, was eager to find a way forward that would enhance the teams' coffers. He sought a solution that would pump up fan interest in teams that had not been in first place prior to the strike. In addition, he foresaw the benefit of invoking a clause in the national TV contract that would allow owners to add another level of playoff games beyond the standard divisional contests. The approach he devised to boost fan interest and maximize team revenue was a "split-season" playoff structure. The teams who had the best record in the East and West Divisions in both leagues when the strike commenced were guaranteed an automatic berth in the playoffs against the second-half winners. What that meant is that the four teams that led their divisions when the strike began on June 12— the New York Yankees and Oakland A's in the American League, and the Philadelphia Phillies and Los Angeles Dodgers in the National League— were suddenly guaranteed in August that they had a chance to win the World Series in October!

The 22 other teams, many of which had been in pennant contention when the strike started, saw any successes in the first half of the season wiped out. When play resumed, all four of the teams that had finished the first half of the season in second place were now tied with the 18 teams below them in the standings whether they had been a half game back or 10 games back. Furthermore, the second-half "winners" would now qualify for the expanded playoffs regardless of their record in the first half.

The scheme gained strong approval from the American League clubs with 12 approving and only the Orioles and White Sox abstaining. They both had good overall records and did not think it was fair to discount their success by starting over. The Orioles' general manager, Hank Peters, wanted to award a playoff spot to the teams with the best overall records (the so-called "Peters Plan"), as everyone had assumed would happen when the strike was resolved. The White Sox proposed that the best second-half team play the team with the best overall record, affording some recognition of performance over the whole season. When that idea gained no traction among the other clubs, Reinsdorf chose to abstain.

In the National League, only the Reds and the Cardinals voted against Kuhn's plan. Both teams were in the pennant chase and they, like the Orioles and the White Sox, did not like the idea of starting over. The Reds' Wagner voiced the club's concern:

> We don't care for the split season for 15-20 reasons, starting with the integrity factor. It's designed to help those clubs that were out of the race. The American League had six teams in the East and four in the West that were contending, and there were six in the National. Integrity? Circumstances could lead a team that won the first half to pick its own opponent, in effect, in the second half. Our fans don't want it.

Wagner then took a sarcastic swipe at the American League's recently adopted designated hitter rule that allowed pitchers not to bat: "We're going to call the guys who took the first half 'the designated winners.'"

The Reds team, along with their fans, were livid. Manager McNamara asked "I think it's horsebleep. Why did we play the first half?"

Second baseman Oester called it a "joke ... especially because the Dodgers played one more game than us." He did not mention that the Dodgers were again scheduled to play one more game than the Reds in the second half. *Cincinnati Enquirer* columnist Tim Sullivan thought the plan was "sinister":

> The possibility exists, and is something less than remote, the best four teams in baseball might not qualify for the playoffs under the sinister split season scheme perpetrated Thursday. In their desire to hype the remainder of this savaged season, baseball's myopic owners have foisted on us a system that rivals the electoral college for stupidity. A system fraught with inequities and fairly dripping with greed. If you did not know that Bowie Kuhn was involved, you would've probably guessed ... Justice, in this case, is deaf and dumb as well as blind ... so why do it? The answer to that, of course, is money. Teams like Houston and Kansas City, which traditionally draw well but have played poorly, have made up in one vote the ground it took them three months to lose. They can now tell their fans to forget the past (and the strike) and think of the great opportunity ahead!

St. Louis Post-Dispatch sports editor Bob Broeg was suspicious of baseball's motives:

> I'd like to bet next year's resolve that, if, say, St. Louis, Baltimore, Milwaukee and maybe Texas had been leading their divisions

at the time of the strike, no such split season would have been declared. After all, those teams wouldn't have created the guaranteed television impact as a playoff in which the first TV market (New York), second (Los Angeles), fourth (Philadelphia), and seventh (Oakland-San Francisco) would assure.

Reds and Cardinals fans were furious. A longtime fan explained:

> We bought season tickets thinking all games would count and now we are told the first half doesn't count, unless you are in Los Angeles? This is a monster created by the owners that makes Frankenstein look like Miss America. A team like Kansas City with a subpar season has a chance to be world champions while our team gets no credit for a great first half? We played one less game, how about at least playing one game against the Dodgers to decide things? I'll take Seaver against Fernando! Those four teams have nothing to play for and can just prepare for the postseason!

A St. Louis fan was equally aghast. "This is a travesty. Why did I buy those season tickets, only to now find out it is as if the games were not played. What a joke!"

When the All-Star Game was played the night before the season resumed on August 10, 7,000 fans returned their tickets. Vice President George H. W. Bush threw out the first pitch. *Cincinnati Enquirer* reporter Randy Holtz opined that it was "fitting because the only big league pitches since June 11 have been thrown by people who also wore three-piece suits."

When the season resumed, Wagner said he was "ready to move on" and "this is the last time in eternity that I will comment on the split season," a pledge he would honor. He did not criticize Kuhn or the owners any further. He was a company man.

John McNamara

"I remember Mr. [Donald] Grant of the Mets saying he was against my selection because the owners were sportsmen, not in it for the money, and that I would seek a bigger slice of the revenue for the players."

MARVIN MILLER
*EXECUTIVE DIRECTOR,
MAJOR LEAGUE BASEBALL PLAYERS ASSOCIATION*

FICTION

15

Day 2 of the Trial

TUESDAY, OCTOBER 6

PRECISELY AT 9:00 A.M., the gavel banged, the clerk called the courtroom to order, and Jackson ascended to his perch. "Good morning. Let's keep this going. Mr. Wright, call your next witness!"

Wright stood and said firmly, "Your Honor, the plaintiffs call Marvin Miller!"

Replied Jackson, "Is Mr. Miller present?"

Miller rose from his seat in the corner. "Yes I am, Your Honor."

"Come forward, please," directed Jackson.

Miller inched his way out of the tenth row of seats, strode up the aisle, opened the swinging doors of the bar that separated the gallery from the trial area of the courtroom, and walked toward the witness stand. He was dressed in a blue sport coat and tan trousers and sported his trademark pencil mustache and slicked-back hair. He looked like an old-style gangster to many, particularly those across the room at MLB's tables.

As he approached, the bailiff intercepted him. "Please raise your right hand." Miller did so. Asked the bailiff, "Do you swear to tell the whole truth and nothing but the truth, so help you God?"

"I do," replied Miller.

"Please be seated and state your full name for the record," said the bailiff.

Miller took his place in the witness box. Looking at Wright and smiling, ever so slightly, he announced: "Marvin Julian Miller."

Wright proceeded to the lectern in center stage. The two men had never met, but Wright had tried to learn as much about Miller as possible in the last 36 hours. Before asking Miller any questions, he elicited background information from Miller, including his previous roles in labor relations.

> Marvin Miller, born in 1917, grew up in Brooklyn as a Dodgers fan. He graduated from college at age 21 with a degree in economics. By 1950, he had held a variety of labor relations jobs as an economist and as a hearing officer adjudicating a wide variety of disputes.
>
> At age 32, he took a job as a staff economist for United Steelworkers of America. The Steelworkers were at the apex of organized labor in postwar America. For the next 16 years, Miller made a name for himself as he pored over government statistics, studied industry trends, and became an expert on cost-of-living figures. Miller's break into the world of baseball came after meeting George Taylor in a San Francisco elevator in December 1966. Taylor had been a labor advisor to every president from Herbert Hoover to the current occupant of the Oval Office, Lyndon Johnson, and he recognized Miller.
>
> Two weeks later, Miller met with three of the four players on the MLB Players Association's search committee: Robin Roberts, Jim Bunning, and Harvey Kuenn. Within a month, Miller was elected to head up

the union after the committee's first choice, Judge Robert Cannon, bowed out because of the low pay. It was controversial among the players to select Miller instead of Cannon precisely because Miller was known as a union man. To many players, there was no place for a real union in baseball. Cubs pitcher Larry Jackson thought a union was as tainted as giving up a game-winning home run. "Let's consider anybody but Miller," he said.

As Miller later recalled, "I remember Mr. [Donald] Grant of the Mets saying he was against my selection because the owners were sportsmen, not in it for the money, and that I would seek a bigger slice of the revenue for the players. Other owners whispered to players about goon squads and strikes and warned them about hiring a labor organizer."

Indeed, the players had reservations of their own. Pitcher Jim Bouton later recounted, "We were all expecting to see someone with a cigar out of the corner of his mouth, a real knuckle-dragging 'deez and doze' guy. Instead, Miller walked in as a quiet, mild, exceedingly understated man." The western teams were swayed by the owners' anti-Miller campaign; when his candidacy was put to an open vote, they rejected him by a margin of 102 to 17. The eastern teams' player reps, having seen the outcome in California and Arizona, made sure to conduct their vote by secret ballot, and Miller prevailed 472 to 34. In March 1966, he was installed as the new executive director of the players association.

Wright asked Miller to describe relations between team owners and the union when he began as executive director. He reported that the union had $5,400 in the bank at the time. Despite the owners' previous promise to contribute $150,000 to the Association's coffers, they failed to do so, citing the Taft-Hartley Act. Testified Miller, "Once I was elected, the owners curiously remembered it would be illegal for employers to fund a union. The owners then refused to negotiate a pension increase, but ultimately we won and the funding was upped by nearly 200 percent. When we started filing grievances over working conditions—everything from warning tracks to hair dryers—the owners refused to meet with us. It backfired." (Disgusted with the owners' intransigence, pitcher Milt Pappas reacted at the time by saying, "Let's go tell them to fuck themselves.'")

Miller went on to describe a series of modest wins achieved by the players in the ensuing years. He told how he and his assistants spent hours meeting with players to talk about pensions, salaries, and the standard contract every player signed. He shared salary information that had previously been withheld by owners. Soon, some players realized that team owners had lied to them about what other players made. For example, Dodgers executive Buzzie Bavasi told Ron Fairly that his contract offer would make Fairly the fourth highest-paid Dodger—behind legends Sandy Koufax, Don Drysdale, and Maury Wills. After Miller presented salary information, Fairly learned he ranked only eighth.

In 1968, Miller negotiated the first collective bargaining agreement with the owners, securing a 42 percent increase in the guaranteed minimum salary as well as establishing an internal arbitration procedure for grievances. Two years later, the owners agreed to have grievances be heard by an independent arbitrator, which was common in most labor agreements in other industries. (This move by Miller would later open the door for arbitrator Seitz's infamous free agency decisions.)

Gradually, the players came around to Miller's take-no-prisoners approach, so much so that they voted to strike before the 1972 season. A couple of weeks into the work stoppage, after being promised greater pension contributions and salary arbitration, Miller had won again. His greatest wins came in the form of the two Seitz decisions that deemed the reserve clause in the standard player contract illegal. As he recounted to the court, the union's victory in achieving free agency ignited a firestorm among the owners.

Wright sensed that a decisive moment in Miller's testimony was approaching. "What happened after the reserve clause was eliminated?" he asked.

"Prior to spring training in 1976, the basic contract agreement between owners and players had expired. When the two sides could not reach an agreement, the owners locked the players out for 17 days of spring training. To get the players back to playing baseball, John Gaherin and I both compromised," Miller said calmly. "He gave me some things we wanted, and I gave MLB a major concession: limited free agency. That meant that players could become free agents only after six years. We thought that would bring peace. Hell, only the best players play more than six years, so most players would never even experience free agency. But that wasn't enough, apparently."

Suddenly, Judge Jackson interrupted the conversation. "Mr. Wright, why is this even important evidence? Aren't we more concerned about the course of events this year?"

Wright was ready. "Your Honor, this is the bedrock of our case. As you know, you are sitting in equity to determine what justice requires if we establish that the defendants broke promises to fans with this contrived split season. We think it is important for the court to have the necessary evidence for us to establish the motive of the owners. Was their decision in the best interests of baseball, or was it in their own best interest?"

Jackson was somewhat unconvinced. "Very well, but let's get moving."

Kuhn nudged Dowd. "Here's your chance. Say something!" Dowd scowled at Kuhn and kept taking notes.

Wright began to get to the main issue. "Mr. Miller, what led us to the strike this year?"

Miller didn't hesitate. "The owners' greed. They claimed free agency would ruin the sport. When they tried to provoke a strike in 1980, we took them up on it because we had decided not to give in to their demands. We had given enough in 1976. The 1980 strike lasted for eight days during spring training."

"What brought the strike to an end?" Wright asked.

"We agreed to set up a committee to study free agency, which effectively kicked the can down the road," Miller replied. "Two owner reps and two players. What they found was that there was no negative effect on baseball from free agency. Attendance and TV ratings increased. Revenues increased. And the owners got richer. But, that wasn't enough for the owners, and we were forced to strike in 1981. If we hadn't, the owners would have continued stripping away free agents' leverage in negotiations."

At this point in the testimony, Wright and Miller were operating like longtime double-play partners. Queried Wright, "Isn't it true that by 1980, pensions were fully funded, per diems had dramatically increased, and players' average annual salary had risen from $19,000 in 1966 to $143,000 per year?

"That's true," Miller said. "Thank you for reminding my members!"

Wright kept going. "When the 1976 lockout was resolved, who won?"

"Most pundits think the union won, but I'll leave that up to historians," Miller replied coolly. "You can ask Mr. Kuhn."

The gallery erupted in laughter. Jackson banged the gavel again. "No more outbursts, or I will close the courtroom to visitors!"

Wright continued, "So, how much money was lost by striking in 1981?"

Answered Miller, "We lost millions and they lost millions during the 51 days of the strike. But they had strike insurance, and we did not. Our members sacrificed a lot of money to maintain the status quo, although we achieved gains to offset losses in the future."

Asked Wright, "Did the owners have a way to recoup lost revenue beyond their insurance policy?"

"No," Miller replied. "And that's why they took the unprecedented action that brought us to this courtroom."

"What do you mean?" asked Wright.

Miller replied, "By creating the split-season playoff format. The owners thought that by wiping away the first-half results, they would promote increased attendance and interest in the second half, because 22 of the 26 teams were now in contention. They were wrong about that, too."

Miller then described how the postseason revenue worked. Players on teams that reached the postseason earned a small share of gate attendance, meaning spectators' ticket revenue. The added round of playoffs might increase total playoff gate attendance because there would be more games for fans to watch, but for the four teams that lost in the first round, the take was very small—approximately 3 percent of the total ticket revenue. Although for those teams the payoff would be better than nothing, the amount each player would get was not all that significant. The players preferred having the regular Championship Series with only four teams, because even the losing teams were promised a far greater share of the gate revenue than they would earn under the modified format.

Then Miller moved on to describe the owners' real moneymaker and the impetus for their desire to have more playoff games: "Although the owners share the gate revenue with players, the bulk of the revenue they hope to take in comes from TV. With an additional round of playoffs, the owners will rake in even more millions from ABC and NBC, revenue that they do not share."

Wright said tersely, "No further questions."

Judge Jackson turned to MLB counsel John Dowd: "Do the defendants care to cross-examine?"

Replied Dowd, "Just a few questions, Your Honor." He continued, "Mr. Miller, did the clubs do anything in violation of the law or the collective bargaining agreement when they adopted the split season?"

Miller, annoyed, said, "No, but it did not give them permission to come up with a screwed up postseason. The agreement says they could split the season, but we never talked about this gimmick."

Retorted Dowd. "So the answer to my question is 'no'"? Miller smirked at Dowd but did not respond. Dowd pressed on. "Very well, did you ask the clubs to negotiate on that subject?"

Miller didn't bite. "No, I read about it in *The New York Times* only after it was announced."

Dowd, going for the jugular, asked, "Did the split season affect the terms you negotiated in any way?"

Miller, in a clipped tone, said, "Not in terms of player compensation!"

Dowd replied curtly, "No further questions."

Judge Jackson looked pointedly at Dowd. "Thank you, Mr. Dowd. It is now past 5:00. The Court will adjourn until 9:00 tomorrow morning. May I see counsel in chambers?"

With that, the US marshals monitoring the proceedings swung the courtroom's doors open, allowing the audience to leave as the lawyers and paralegals huddled. Kuhn cornered Dowd: "What the hell was that about? Three questions? John, whose side are you on!?"

Dowd glared at Kuhn. "Are you going to second-guess me like you did Gaherin and Grebey? Am I next to be fired? There was nothing Miller could say to help us except what I asked him. I'm not wasting the judge's time. Why don't you wait outside until we talk to the judge? Have everyone stay and we'll talk over dinner."

The two principals retreated to the judge's chambers on the second floor of the courthouse. As is customary, Jackson wanted to know what to expect the next day. Wright explained that Grebey would be called as the next witness. Jackson then turned to Dowd. "Wouldn't the simple solution be to add a few teams and create another round? Give the Reds and Cardinals home field advantage to make up for this?"

Dowd was taken aback. He had not considered any change as an option. "Judge, that would be ridiculous. We'd be pushing the postseason into November. The World Series can't be played fairly in November if northern teams participate. The weather would be too bad."

The judge then encouraged both sides to try to settle the case. Jackson, like Moffett before him, was hoping the sides could work it out. "Mr. Dowd, give Mr. Wright a call after you talk to Mr. Kuhn. I'll check with you in the morning. Then we can get on with the games."

Kuhn and Dowd huddled with the TV executives in their suite at the Hotel LeVeque after a conference call with a group of owners. The hotel, a landmark art deco high-rise overlooking the Scioto River, was just blocks from the courthouse. Befitting the owners, it was an elegant, upscale hotel across the street from the Ohio Statehouse.

Kuhn broke the news to the TV execs. "Gentlemen, tomorrow is

Wednesday. Even if we get a favorable decision by then, there's no way to hold games on Wednesday night or even Thursday. The owners just voted to push the games until Friday."

The group was upset. ABC's VP, John Bogusz, was the first to respond, directing his questions at Dowd. "John, how did we not see this coming? Is there any way to settle this? Can't we just substitute Cincinnati in the playoffs or buy the Plaintiffs lifetime passes to the World Series?"

Dowd recounted the conversation with the judge. "He's thinking like you. Judges love cases to settle so they don't have to make hard decisions."

Kuhn was nonplussed by any settlement talk. "We have lost to the players for the last 15 years. We'll have a mutiny if we suggest anything like that. I have every confidence that Dowd will turn this around."

Meanwhile at Mehlman's Pub, the boys were having dinner with Wright and going over the outline for Grebey's cross-examination the next day. Opey approached the table. "Mr. Wright, there's a Mr. Dowd on the phone for you." Wright was surprised, having told the boys the owners would never settle. He went to the bar and picked up the phone. "Hello, John. I'm glad I gave you this number. Any progress with your client?"

Dowd replied, "I had to call you or the judge would be pissed at me. But you know we can't settle this thing."

As the chief competition for the second-half NL West crown emerges, the Reds begin their playoff push out west against an old friend.

16
The Second-Half Folly

ONCE A DEAL WAS STRUCK between the players' union and team owners, teams had less than two weeks to prepare for the second half of the 1981 season. The All-Star Game in Cleveland, won 5-4 by the National League, marked the beginning of the post-strike season, as teams resumed play the very next day.

For the Reds, the second half ironically began on the West Coast versus the despised Dodgers, beneficiaries of Kuhn's split-season decree because they had played one more game (and notched one more win) in the first half of the season than the second-place Reds. Unfortunately, Reds starter Frank Pastore couldn't make it to the third inning, yielding four earned runs and five hits. The Reds' offense was shut down by Jerry Reuss and Steve Howe. Cincinnati managed just three hits and moved only one runner into scoring position.

The Reds wound up losing two out of three in LA, then had a day off before playing four games in three days versus the Giants. The clubs were forced to play two games on August 14 to make up for a rainout on May 26. In the first contest, the Reds' bats again went cold. Ed Whitson, an All-Star in 1980 with San Francisco, blanked the Reds over nine innings. Cincinnati claimed the second game when Sam Mejias singled in George Foster in the 10th inning for a 7-6 victory. Mejias, a backup outfielder, had given Griffey a rest in the nightcap. Batting leadoff for the Giants in both games of the double dip was none other than Joe Morgan, who was in his first season with San Francisco.

> Born in Bonham, Texas, Joe Morgan moved to Oakland with his family when he was five. Fourteen years later, the Houston Colt .45s—the franchise that became the Astros in 1964—signed Morgan for $500 a month and a $3,000 signing bonus. Morgan received his first taste of the majors in 1963 as a September call-up when rosters expanded. He debuted two days after his 20th birthday and after only 140 outings in the minors. In 1964, Morgan was again a September call-up before sticking in the majors for good in 1965.
>
> Short in stature but long in patience at the plate, Morgan was runner-up in the NL Rookie of the Year voting in 1965. He made his first of 10 All-Star appearances in 1966, when he hit .285 with an impressive .410 on-base percentage. With the exception of the 1968 season when he was injured for all but 10 games, Morgan excelled as Houston's regular second baseman through 1971. Apart from Pete Rose and Don Buford, Morgan accumulated the most wins above replacement (WAR) among all MLB second basemen from 1965 to 1971. (WAR measures a player's value by quantifying how many more wins he's worth than a replacement-level player at his same position.) Morgan liked playing in Houston, but he had a frosty relationship with manager Harry Walker. Morgan reportedly thought Walker was a racist; Walker thought Morgan was a troublemaker.

On November 29, 1971, Morgan, along with Cesar Geronimo, Jack Billingham, Ed Armbrister and Denis Menke—all of whom would go on to play roles with the Big Red Machine—were traded to Cincinnati for Tommy Helms, Lee May, and Jimmy Stewart. The swap was one of the most lopsided trades in baseball history. The trade provided the Machine with a fourth star (Morgan) to pair with Bench, Perez, and Rose; a Gold Glove center fielder (Geronimo); and a linchpin of the Reds' rotation for the next six seasons (Billingham). But the clear prize was Morgan, whose game immediately took off in the Queen City. In 1972, Morgan paced the NL in runs, walks, and on-base percentage, and he began a streak of making eight straight NL All-Star teams. Morgan earned the first of five straight Gold Gloves in 1973, but by 1975 he had become arguably the best player in baseball, turning in one of the finest seasons in baseball history.

In 1975, at age 31, Morgan led the majors in walks (132) and on-base percentage (a ridiculous .466). He hit .327 and drove in 94 runs. In 639 plate appearances, Morgan struck out only 52 times. He was the near-unanimous choice (96%) for the first of what would be back-to-back NL MVP awards. But maybe the most impressive statistic for Morgan in 1975? 11. That was how many wins above replacement he racked up. Since 1975, only Barry Bonds (twice), Roger Clemens, and Pedro Martinez have posted better single-season WAR totals, as recorded by *Baseball Reference*. "I have never seen anyone, and I mean anyone, play better than Joe has played this year," Sparky Anderson said during the season. Morgan's bloop single plated the go-ahead run in Game 7 of the World Series.

Morgan was almost as good in 1976, again leading

> the majors in WAR (9.6) and on-base percentage (.444). He set career bests in home runs (27) and RBI (111). After stealing 67 bases in 1975, Morgan stole 60 in 1976. In the World Series versus the Yankees, Morgan hit .333 with a .412 on-base percentage in 17 plate appearances. Though he never again reached the improbable heights of 1975 and 1976, Morgan remained productive throughout the rest of his career. He returned to Houston for a year in 1980 before spending the next two seasons with the Giants, winning NL Comeback Player of the Year in 1982 along with a Silver Slugger Award. Morgan linked up with Rose and Perez on the 1983 Phillies and reached the World Series one final time. On September 30, 1984, Morgan, age 41, played his last game, doubling in his final at-bat while playing for the Oakland Athletics. Among second basemen, only three players—and none since Jackie Robinson broke the sport's color barrier in 1947—have accumulated more WAR than Morgan: Rogers Hornsby, Eddie Collins, and Nap Lajoie. Morgan was elected to the National Baseball Hall of Fame in 1990, and in 1998 the Reds retired Morgan's number 8 jersey. Morgan died at age 77 in October 2020.

Morgan started and led off the third game of the series, too, going hitless in a Giants victory. However, the Reds claimed the last contest of the series 2-1 behind a combined pitching gem from Soto (6.1 innings, one run, six strikeouts) and Tom Hume (2.2 innings, seventh save), the first of four successive wins. Cincinnati closed the month with a record of only 4-6, leaving them with a 10-10 record in August, a mark they were fortunate to reach considering they were outscored by 26 runs.

The .500 start wasn't ideal given the new format: finish first in the NL West or go home. But, unlike the first half of 1981, Cincinnati's foremost foe for first place would not come from Los Angeles, but from Houston. At the end of August, the Reds were fourth in the NL West, 2.5 games behind Houston, two games back of San Francisco, and a game and a half behind both Atlanta and Los Angeles. The Astros raced to a 13-8 start in the second half, sending a shot across the bow to the Reds. Based on the August results, there was a legitimate chance of a four-team race to the finish for the second-half NL West crown. (The Padres, 10 games under .500 in the first half, were 5-17 in August.)

Houston won five straight at the end of August and tacked on four more victories to start September largely as the result of seemingly indomitable pitching. The starting rotation was led by Nolan Ryan, who would go on to win the majors' ERA title (1.69) in 21 starts. In second behind Ryan was another Astro and first-time All-Star, Bob Knepper. In his first year with Houston following five seasons with San Francisco, Knepper recorded a 2.18 ERA in 22 starts, despite striking out just 75 batters in 156.2 innings. The rest of the rotation was locked down by a pair of 36-year-olds in Don Sutton (2.61 ERA in 23 starts) and Joe Niekro (2.82 ERA in 24 starts), as well as Vern Ruhle, who started 15 of the 20 games he pitched in and notched a 2.91 ERA. Like Knepper, Ruhle found success sans the strikeout (39 Ks in 102 innings). In addition to its impressive team ERA, Houston finished 1981 with the most strikeouts while surrendering the fewest hits in the National League.

Rose's Phillies were slow out of the gate (7-13) in August, though having already secured the first-half NL East title, the club had little to play for besides keeping a lid on injuries. After nearly two months of waiting to break Musial's NL hits record, Rose wasted no time in making history, hitting an opposite-field single in the eighth inning of the Phillies' first game back. As luck would have it, his record breaker came against St. Louis, the only club Musial had played for in his 22-year career. Musial was on hand to congratulate Rose. (In one of life's strange twists, Musial had delivered his final two hits on September 29, 1963, against the Reds and their rookie, Pete Rose.)

NL WEST STANDINGS THROUGH AUGUST

Team	Wins	Losses	Ties	W/L %	Games Back
Houston Astros	13	8	0	.619	—
San Francisco Giants	12	8	0	.600	0.5
Atlanta Braves	12	9	0	.571	1.0
Los Angeles Dodgers*	11	9	0	.550	1.0
Cincinnati Reds	10	10	0	.500	2.5
San Diego Padres	5	17	0	.227	8.5

*Already qualified for the postseason. No incentive to win.

NL EAST STANDINGS THROUGH AUGUST

Team	Wins	Losses	Ties	W/L %	Games Back
St. Louis Cardinals	12	6	0	.667	—
Montreal Expos	11	8	0	.579	1.5
Chicago Cubs	11	10	0	.524	2.5
New York Mets	11	10	0	.524	2.5
Philadelphia Phillies*	7	13	0	.350	6.0
Pittsburgh Pirates	7	15	0	.318	7.0

* Already qualified for the postseason. No incentive to win.

AL WEST STANDINGS THROUGH AUGUST

Team	Wins	Losses	Ties	W/L %	Games Back
Oakland Athletics*	10	9	0	.526	—
Chicago White Sox	10	10	0	.500	0.5
Kansas City Royals	10	11	0	.476	1.0
California Angels	9	10	0	.474	1.0
Texas Rangers	9	10	0	.474	1.0
Minnesota Twins	9	13	0	.409	2.5
Seattle Mariners	8	13	0	.381	3.0

*Already qualified for the postseason. No incentive to win.

AL EAST STANDINGS THROUGH AUGUST

Team	Wins	Losses	Ties	W/L %	Games Back
Detroit Tigers	13	8	0	.619	—
Milwaukee Brewers	13	9	0	.591	0.5
Baltimore Orioles	11	9	0	.550	1.5
Boston Red Sox	11	9	0	.550	1.5
New York Yankees*	11	10	0	.524	2.0
Toronto Blue Jays	9	10	0	.474	3.0
Cleveland Indians	10	12	0	.455	3.5

* Already qualified for the postseason. No incentive to win.

"It was claimed that I said the owners' strategy was, 'Fuck you, because I'm stronger, because I'm richer, and because I can beat you.' I never said that was the owners' strategy."

RAY GREBEY
MLB'S CHIEF LABOR NEGOTIATOR

17

Day 3 of the Trial

WEDNESDAY, OCTOBER 7

PROMPTLY AT 9:00 A.M., Judge Jackson entered the courtroom. The courtroom was again overflowing. After having conferred with his law clerks for the previous 90 minutes, he was still uncertain as to whether he should intervene in MLB's playoffs and disrupt the postseason.

Looking at Wright and Dowd, he asked, "Gentlemen, anything to report this morning?" Jackson was coy, not wanting to alert the gallery that he had encouraged a settlement.

Dowd stood. "Nothing, Your Honor." Jackson frowned. He was not surprised, as he speculated that MLB did not want to negotiate.

"Very well. Mr. Wright, call your next witness."

Wright stood quickly: "We call Raymond Grebey, as if on cross-examination." Wright's reference to "cross-examination" signaled to the judge that Wright expected Grebey to be a hostile witness, which would give Wright more leeway when asking questions. No one objected.

Grebey knew that he was going to be the first witness that morning, so he was seated in the first row behind Dowd. He advanced to the witness chair, took the oath, and sat down. He was dressed in tweeds and a Chicago Cubs tie, making him look more like a professor than what he was: a corporate executive. His trademark pipe was visible inside his coat pocket.

Grebey looked directly at Wright as Wright approached the lectern. Without prompting, Grebey announced himself. "Clarence Raymond Grebey, Junior."

> **Ray Grebey grew up on the north side of Chicago as a Cubs fan, and his family had season tickets at Wrigley Field. He had never witnessed a World Series there. Grebey, 53, was a graduate of Kenyon College and the University of Chicago, where he obtained his MBA degree. After serving in the Korean War, he spent 20 years at General Electric, where he rose to second in command of labor relations before joining MLB.**

After exchanging "good mornings," Wright quickly got Grebey to concede his reputation was that of a "union buster."

Said Grebey, "That is my reputation, but that is not who I am. In fact, you are well aware of my landmark affirmative action case a couple years ago, and we discarded Boulwarism years ago." (He was talking about the "take it or leave it" negotiating strategy adopted by Lemuel Boulware, GE's chief labor negotiator in the 1960s.) He added, "I am an enlightened bargainer. I prefer win-win solutions."

Wright countered, "But weren't you hired because the owners thought your predecessor, Mr. Gaherin, had made too many concessions to the Players Association?"

"That's probably fair," Grebey relented.

Wright stepped closer to Grebey as he asked, "In fact, you recently said that the owners' strategy was based on a three-legged stool. Explain that."

An irritated Grebey said, "That's not fair. You know I said I was misquoted."

Asked Wright: "How were you quoted?"

Dowd stood again. "Objection! He said he was misquoted."

Jackson interjected, "So? Overruled. Mr. Grebey. You're allowed to explain, but first answer the question."

Grebey, annoyed, said, "Some claimed that I said the owners' strategy was, 'Fuck you, because I'm stronger, because I'm richer, and because I can beat you.' I never said that was the owners' strategy."

Dowd looked at Grebey with dismay. *You basically just lied to the court. Of course you said that. I told you to just accept bad facts, but not to lie. This is exactly why you will not negotiate another contract.* Kuhn mouthed *"what the hell?"* to Dowd. Dowd shook his head. All the while, Jackson was watching.

Wright then methodically walked Grebey through the timeline of his hiring by MLB. Gaherin had been fired after the 1976 bargaining because the owners thought he gave in to players' demands too easily. Grebey was hired in 1978 to replace him. The owners took Grebey's advice to buy strike insurance before the 1980 negotiations.

"Had the owners ever purchased strike insurance before?" asked Wright.

Grebey replied, "No."

"They were planning on a strike, correct?" Wright queried.

Grebey conceded, "We knew it was possible."

Wright continued to suggest that Kuhn had instructed Grebey to get more compensation for teams who lost free agents. He said that in 1979, when Kuhn mentioned that idea to Miller for the first time, the latter said, "They'll get compensation over my dead body." Wright explained that Grebey and Miller bargained fruitlessly up to the 1980 strike deadline, at which point the two of them agreed to set up a committee to discuss the free agent compensation issue. That joint decision, said Wright, averted the 1980 strike.

Asked Wright, "Mr. Grebey, when you and Mr. Miller reached this agreement in 1980, you called a press conference, correct?"

Answered Grebey, "Yes."

"And during that press conference you claimed victory?" posed Wright.

Grebey replied emphatically: "No."

Dowd was beside himself. *Yes you did, you son of a bitch. I told you to admit things. Don't lie.*

Wright went in for the kill. "Okay, Mr. Grebey, you just said under oath that you did not declare victory during that press conference. What did you say to the press?"

Grebey replied, "All I said was that our proposal for compensation could not be removed without agreement of both parties. It was inartfully worded. But the union needed to give a strike notice to avoid that part of the deal."

Wright then walked to the counsel table, and Chase, his co-counsel, handed him a one-page document. "May I approach the witness, Your Honor?" asked Wright.

"Certainly," replied Jackson.

Wright looked pointedly at Grebey as he handed him the document after providing a copy to Judge Jackson and to Dowd. "Mr. Grebey, I was mistaken. You did not call a press conference. Instead, you issued a press release. And in that press release you wrote, 'In 1981, the Clubs' proposal for compensation becomes a part of the Basic Agreement and it cannot be removed without agreement of the two sides.' Is it fair to say you were intending to claim victory?"

Dowd rose again. "Objection. The document speaks for itself."

For once, Jackson agreed with Dowd and sustained the objection. Jackson then turned to Grebey: "Mr. Grebey, that press release misrepresented your deal, isn't that right? You could not impose your compensation proposal without the players agreeing, right?"

Grebey replied, "Not exactly. We could only do that if they did not give us a strike notice within the required amount of time."

Jackson continued, "How likely was it that Mr. Miller would miss that deadline?"

Said Grebey, "Not very likely."

"Thank you," said the judge.

Dowd was livid again. *Grebey thought he could fool the judge? We've been through this before. Just answer the questions and don't worry about where Wright is going. That is better than evading the question. Or, worse, lying.*

Proceeding with his questioning, Wright reviewed the events that occurred after the ill-fated press release went out. Thanks to the boys' research, he was aware that up to 20 owners had phoned Grebey after Miller organized his own press conference and called Grebey a liar. Grebey's response was that he rushed the release, but that Miller was upset only because Grebey came up with a good quote first. *The New York Times* quoted Grebey as saying, "Marvin just couldn't take someone else getting a better quote. It's like a guy who's hit 30 straight home runs and then you strike him out."

Wright went for the jugular: "Mr. Grebey, by your analogy, is Mr. Miller the guy who hit the home runs and then you struck him out with an illegal spitball?

Grebey did not respond, but the point was made. Grebey had lied to the press about the one and only issue that led to the 1981 strike and the resulting split-season format.

Jackson threw Grebey a lifeline. "The court notes that we have been going for almost three hours. We will adjourn for an early lunch. Let's resume at 1:15 p.m."

In the hallway, Kuhn looked despairingly at Dowd. "How do we regain credibility?"

Dowd looked down at his polished shoes. "We sure as hell need him off the stand. It's up to you to convince the judge. These are all red herrings. We can design playoffs anyway we want to. It's that simple. This is all bullshit."

When court resumed after lunch, Wright continued his cross-examination of Grebey. "In one of your mediation sessions with the players and Mr. Moffett, do you recall that the player reps were wearing clothing that referred to you?" The question was designed to bring the judge's attention back to the pre-lunch line of questioning.

Grebey replied, "Yes. It was insulting. The players wore T-shirts printed with the words 'Grebey: TRUST ME.' Marvin put them up to it."

Asked Wright, "So it appears the players did not trust you. How about the owners who hired you? Is it correct that there was dissension among the owners about your strategy before the strike?"

Grebey knew what Wright was asking. But instead of answering the question, he tried to figure out how the plaintiffs' lawyer had all this inside information. Was the union helping the plaintiffs? Were some of the owners helping them? Lawyers who prepare witnesses to give testimony always give this advice, "Don't try to figure out where the lawyer is going. Just answer the question. We will have an opportunity to tell our story." But Grebey didn't take that time-tested advice and instead made a classic mistake. "I don't know what you are talking about," he said. "We were united. We all know professional baseball is in danger if we don't change the free agency rules."

Wright then laid out a number of examples of how the owners had not been unified in the way they wanted to respond to the union's demands. Wright first described how Grebey had arranged for the $50-million strike insurance policy from Lloyd's of London. He then solicited $15 million in contributions from the teams for a "mutual protection fund" and imposed a gag order on the owners throughout negotiations. Silencing a group of 26 men who are used to getting their way proved to be difficult, particularly when there was so much at stake. Harry Dalton, general manager of the Milwaukee Brewers, thought he was having an off-the-record conversation with *Washington Post* writer Tom Boswell. Dalton told Boswell, "I hope that we are not about to witness another macho test of wills. From what I hear, the Players Association is genuinely looking for a compromise if we'll just offer them something that they can accept without losing too much face." Dalton was fined $50,000 by MLB for violating the gag order, but he never paid it.

Baltimore Orioles owner Ed Williams warned his fellow owners that they were fighting Miller on the wrong issue. "You've got to fight this on something other than Marvin's monument of free agency." Williams had some support among the other owners, but most were hardliners who were willing to go to the mat on the issue of teams being compensated for losing free agents.

Finally, Brewers owner Ed Fitzgerald screamed at Williams during a particularly contentious meeting in mid-July. "We've had enough of your shit. Now sit down and shut up."

Ted Turner of the Braves was also in a fighting spirit: "That gimpy-armed Jew bastard [referring to Miller]. We'll run him out of town once and for all." (Miller had a withered right arm as the result of a birth defect.)

Grebey should have known by now that Wright knew the answer to his question before he asked it. There was plenty of dissension among the owners, and Grebey had done his best to try and skirt the issue. Still, Grebey was not being completely misleading about the owners being unified. After all, they all shared the same objective of protecting their bottom line. If anything, Grebey was guilty only of exaggeration.

Wright was nearly finished. He had wanted to capture the owners' hostility toward the union and lay bare Grebey's lack of credibility. He had accomplished both goals. Only one objective remained. "Mr. Grebey, when did the owners decide to effectively end the strike?"

Replied Grebey, "July 31."

Queried Wright, "When the strike insurance ran out?"

Grebey shrugged. "Basically."

Wright paused before wrapping up the cross-examination: "One final question. When your family bought season tickets for the Cubs, were you guaranteed rights to purchase postseason tickets?"

Grebey reluctantly conceded: "Yes."

Replied Wright, "And is that one of the reasons you bought the tickets?"

Said Grebey with a smile, "You know well and good that the Cubs don't make the postseason!"

Laughter erupted from the gallery and from Judge Jackson, but Wright's point had been made. Seizing the moment, Wright said, "No further questions, Your Honor. With that, we rest our case."

Dowd wanted time to huddle with Kuhn and his team of lawyers. "Your Honor, we think it best to adjourn for a few hours so we can prepare our defense and end the proceedings as soon as possible. We suggest a break until the morning."

Jackson responded, "Your call. I know you realize the urgency. We will adjourn until nine in the morning. We will then start the defendant's case with Mr. Grebey. Mr. Grebey, you are still under oath, and I admonish you not to discuss the specifics of your testimony with anyone until you are released from the witness stand. We have yet to hear your direct testimony."

Judge Jackson turned to Dowd: "Any witnesses besides Mr. Grebey?

Replied Dowd, "Just one more. Commissioner Bowie Kuhn will be called after Mr. Grebey."

"Very well," said the judge. "See you bright and early."

The bailiff slammed the gavel, and the courtroom emptied rather quickly. To courtroom observers, Judge Jackson seemed increasingly interested in the two sides' sticking points that had led to the strike and the resulting playoff modification. Like many fans and nonfans alike, he thought professional baseball players made an awful lot of money just for playing a game. In fact, many of them made more than he did, and he was a federal judge with years of education and experience! But, as inquiring minds had observed, he had asked only a few questions, which worried both sides. Had he already made up his mind?

George Grande was back on ESPN with a live update. "I never thought I'd say this, but the lawyer for the fans is well-prepared. He seems to have inside information, because we are hearing things in the federal courtroom in Columbus that we have not heard before. Commissioner Kuhn will take the stand tomorrow, and he better be prepared to explain his split-season decision. For now, there will be no games until Friday at the earliest. And maybe the Reds and Cardinals ought to start warming up. Everything is up in the air! We'll be back at 10 tonight with an hour-long special edition of *SportsCenter* called 'Baseball Trial of the Century.'"

An instant Nielsen ratings sample saw ESPN viewership spike. Stuart Evey grinned.

The Reds finish with baseball's best record but are left out of the rejiggered postseason.

18
The Second Half Ends

THE REDS' HOPES FOR A POSTSEASON BERTH were on the line as the 1981 calendar flipped to September. They split their first eight games, but even their losses included thrilling baseball. The fun began on September 9 when Cincinnati claimed the first triumph in what would be three successive last-at-bat wins at Riverfront Stadium. That trio of victories pushed the Reds' second half record to 17-14, three games back of the Astros. The Big Red Machine powered the first win. Trailing the Padres 4-2 in the ninth, Griffey brought the home team within one with a run-scoring groundout. Then, Concepción tied the game with a single. After Foster walked, Bench—who had returned from injury on August 26, but didn't make his first start (at first base) until September 3—singled to center field to score Concepción. The next night against Los Angeles, Cincinnati wasted seven innings of two-run ball by Soto only to have Ron Oester save the day with a homer to right field off Alejandro Pena in the bottom of the 10th inning. On September 11, Concepción's sacrifice fly off Ted Power in the bottom of the 11th secured another important decision over the Dodgers.

After dropping the series finale versus Los Angeles, the Reds embarked on a grueling stretch, easily one of the most demanding road trips the franchise had ever undertaken: a 13-game, 14-day, 5-city journey from September 14 through 27. Just one of the cities was in the Eastern time zone, and three of the series were in California. The Reds were barely ahead of the Giants (17-15) and were in danger of losing ground and fast—to the Dodgers (20-14) and the red-hot Astros (22-11).

Stop No. 1: Houston. Cincinnati had little reason to fear Houston despite the latter's intimidating pitching. The Reds were 5-3 against the Astros and had scored 28 runs in those eight games. They had already beaten Nolan Ryan and Don Sutton. Bench, Concepción, Griffey, and Foster were not in their prime, but they were still capable of inflicting damage on top-tier pitchers. And that's exactly what happened in the first game of the Reds' 13-game road trip. Griffey (two hits), Concepción (three hits) and Bench (three hits, three RBI) carried Cincinnati in a 4-2 victory. Starter Bruce Berenyi, who went on to place fourth in the voting for the National League's Rookie of the Year, went the distance on the mound for the visitors, striking out 12.

The next night, the Reds drew Ryan, and incredibly, the Ryan Express was outdueled by another unfamiliar Cincinnati starter. Charlie Leibrandt, like Berenyi before him, notched a nine-inning shutout for his only victory of the season. In fact, Leibrandt pitched only 30 innings total for the Reds all year. In this outing, Leibrandt scattered five hits, walked three, and fanned four. Offensively, it was Foster's turn to play run producer, driving in two. By winning two games in the Astrodome, the Reds climbed to 19-15 and were just 2.5 games out of first place. Off to San Francisco.

The first game against the Giants was a forgettable one. Soto was shelled (four runs, one out recorded) in a 12-7 defeat. The second game was a nail-biter. On September 17, Seaver and San Francisco starter Ed

Whitson combined for 17 scoreless innings. The Reds got going in the top of the 10th versus Al Holland, with Paul Householder and Griffey opening the frame with back-to-back hits to put runners at second and third. Greg Minton replaced Holland and was greeted with a run-scoring single by Concepción. Tom Hume made the lead stand in the bottom half of the inning. On to Los Angeles.

In the first foray of the teams' three-game series, the Dodgers led 3-1 in the seventh inning. But then the lesser-knowns rallied the Reds. After catcher Joe Nolan doubled off Bob Welch with two outs, Oester singled in Nolan, the Reds' primary catcher in 1981. (Nolan started at catcher in 62 of the team's 81 games, hitting .309). Following a single by Larry Biittner, Steve Howe was brought in to face Dave Collins, who delivered a base hit to score Oester. LA went ahead by one in the home half of the eighth, but Bench popped a two-run, pinch-hit homer to put the Reds ahead 5-4 in the ninth, and the lead would last. And Cincinnati wasn't finished torturing the Dodgers. Over their final two games in LA, the Reds racked up 12 runs and 24 hits in a pair of wins, receiving offensive contributions from up and down the roster. At 23-16, Cincinnati had moved into second place in the NL West, 2.5 games behind Houston.

The four-game win streak came to a screeching halt in the Reds' first game in San Diego, thanks to Chris Welsh, who tossed a complete-game shutout. But the Reds got back to their winning ways the next day behind seven-plus strong innings from Seaver and three hits from Foster. After Joe Price gave up a double and a walk to lead off the inning, Hume took the mound. The Padres bunted the runners over. Hume intentionally walked Tim Flannery before initiating a 6-4-3 double play to end the game. In the series finale in San Diego, Cincinnati struck early via run-scoring hits from Foster and backup infielder Junior Kennedy. They never looked back, winning 5-1. Frank Pastore pitched successfully into the eighth.

The Reds finally had a day off on September 24 as they made their way to Atlanta, the final leg of their trip. So far, they were 7-2. Unfortunately for the Reds, as soon as they left Houston in the middle of the month, the Astros had quickly rediscovered their mojo, winning five of six. As the Reds began their three-game series in Atlanta, they still sat 2.5 games behind Houston.

In the first game opposite the Braves, Cincinnati dominated offensively and on the mound. The Reds scored multiple runs in four of the first seven innings and accumulated 14 hits in the 10-2 decision. Soto was masterful, supplying yet another complete-game outing. Remember Berenyi? He blanked Atlanta over seven innings in a 2-0 win on September 26. In the getaway game, Ken Griffey's three-run double in the second inning was enough offense for Seaver (five innings) and Mike LaCoss (four innings). Incredibly, the Reds returned to Cincinnati having won 11 of 13 over their 14-day excursion. Their cumulative record of 62-38 for the season was the best in baseball, and they were just a game and a half behind the Astros in the NL West. Cincinnati had just seven games left to overtake Houston— and all of them would take place at Riverfront Stadium.

Less than two weeks after splitting a pair of contests in San Francisco, the Reds and the Giants repeated a split on September 28 and 29 in Cincinnati. San Francisco blanked the hosts 4-0 in the first game, a crucial loss for the Reds since the Astros won in the bottom of the ninth over San Diego. Cincinnati won in walk-off style themselves the next night. With the score tied in the ninth, Foster and Bench led off with a double and a single, respectively. After Knight's attempted sacrifice bunt resulted in Foster being thrown out at third base, Oester saved the day once more with a run-scoring single, plating pinch runner Rafael Landestoy. The Astros lost 2-1, inching the Reds to 1.5 games back of first but with few opportunities left to gain ground.

Fortunately for Cincinnati, Houston was coming to town for two games. The Reds hoped two victories would put them in first place for good.

A surprisingly small crowd of 24,394 attended the first game. The Reds trailed for the first four and a half innings before striking in the fifth, sixth, and seventh innings. Foster homered in the fifth to tie the game. Collins and Concepción tallied run-scoring hits in the sixth, with Knight and Oester doing the same in the seventh. Soto was excellent on the mound, spinning eight innings of two-run ball. With a 5-2 victory to cap a 20-8 record in September, Cincinnati was just a half-game back of first place in the NL West.

Having spent over a decade with the Reds, Foster was well-versed in division title chases. However, his path toward being an indispensable slugger for Cincinnati was a well-traveled one that required years of patience.

Drafted by the San Francisco Giants in the third round of the 1968 draft, George Foster spent the next season and a half terrorizing A-ball pitching, so much so that the Giants called him up to finish the 1969 season. Foster's first major league appearance was on September 10, when, at age 20, he replaced his boyhood hero, Willie Mays, in the eighth inning as a defensive substitute.

Foster spent much of the 1970 season at Triple-A before he was once again a late-September call-up to the Giants. He made the big-league club as a reserve outfielder in 1971, but he wasn't around for long. On May 29, in what would prove to be one of the most lopsided trades in Reds history, Foster was traded to Cincinnati for light-hitting shortstop Frank Duffy and minor league pitcher Vern Geishert. Because of an injury to Bobby Tolan, Foster gained ample playing time upon his arrival,

but he hit only .234 with 10 home runs and had an OPS of .675 in 104 games. Foster famously scored the winning run in the 1972 NLCS versus Pittsburgh, but it was an otherwise forgettable season with his new organization, as he appeared in just 59 games. Foster was sent down to Triple-A Indianapolis to start the 1973 season. Though initially disappointed at the demotion, Foster's newfound friendship with Ken Griffey helped him rediscover the joy of baseball. Foster again garnered a late-season call-up with the Reds, but he was ineligible to play in the NLCS.

In 1974, Foster played his way into a roster spot, but he was stuck behind Griffey, Rose, and Geronimo in the outfield pecking order. He hit .264 in 106 games playing in a part-time role, but by 1975, his improvement was evident. Rose moved from left field to third base, opening up an outfield role for Foster, then age 26. Foster took full advantage of the opportunity, hitting .300 in 134 games. He also hit 23 home runs—second on the team behind Johnny Bench—drove in 78 runs, and played excellent outfield defense (just three errors). Foster thrived in the playoffs, registering 12 hits in 42 plate appearances. In the Reds' extra-inning loss in Game 6 of the World Series against Boston, Foster threw out the potential winning run in the bottom of the ninth. He also caught Carlton Fisk's iconic game-winning home run ball after it struck the left-field foul pole in the bottom of the 12th inning.

With the Reds gunning for a second straight world championship in 1976, Foster turned in his best season. He hit .306 with a .364 on-base percentage, swatting a team-high 29 homers and driving in an MLB-high 121 runs. Foster not only made his first of what would be four successive All-Star teams, he walloped a two-run homer off Catfish Hunter, earning MVP honors in the game. For the season, he finished second in MVP voting behind teammate Joe Morgan, having stockpiled 5.9 wins above replacement (WAR) in 1976. Foster struggled in the NLCS against the Phillies, but he crushed the Yankees' pitching in the World Series, hitting .429 in the Reds' four-game sweep. Though the Reds missed the postseason in 1977, Foster enjoyed the best season of his career en route to winning National League MVP. He established a pair of team records that stand to this day with 52 home runs and 149 runs batted in, both of which led the majors, along with his 388 total bases, .613 slugging percentage, and outrageous 1.013 OPS. Foster's 52 bombs were the most home runs in a single season since Mays clubbed 52 in 1965, and he amassed a ridiculous 8.4 WAR. Foster also put together strong campaigns in 1978 (.281 average, 40 HRs, 120 RBI) and 1979 (.302 average, 30 HRs, 98 RBI in 121 games).

After another solid season in 1980, Foster picked up his fifth and final All-Star nod in 1981. He drove in 90 runs while playing all 108 games, his sixth successive season with at least 90 RBI. Finishing third in the NL MVP voting behind Mike Schmidt and Andre Dawson, Foster hit .295 with 22 round-trippers. In February 1982, Foster was traded to the New York Mets for three players. With the Mets, he notched 99 home runs in four-plus seasons.

Unfortunately for the Reds, Nolan Ryan rose up in the October 1 matchup and the Reds had no answer. Fresh off his fifth career no-hitter, the 34-year-old quieted the Machine and the rest of the Reds' offense in an 8-1 Houston victory, fanning nine in a complete-game effort. With the Astros leaving town for three games in Los Angeles, Cincinnati required assistance from its bitter rivals—already safely in the postseason, remember—if they were to preserve their playoff hopes. As it turns out, the Reds, who welcomed the free-falling Braves for three games, should have focused more on helping themselves.

In the first game against Atlanta, the Reds' pitching staff picked the worst possible night to submit one of their most lackluster showings of the season. Frank Pastore started and didn't make it out of the fourth inning, allowing five runs. Paul Moskau relieved Pastore and dumped a tanker of gasoline on the fire, yielding five hits and five runs while recording just two outs. Cincinnati's offense managed five runs off 42-year-old Gaylord Perry, but Atlanta's 14 hits put them on top in an 11-5 decision. Fortunately for the Reds, the Dodgers dropped the Astros 6-1. In order to finish with the best second-half record in the NL West, the Reds needed Los Angeles to win the final two games of the series and take care of their own business against the Braves.

Saturday, October 3, 1981. The Reds' penultimate game of the 1981 regular season would determine whether they would move on to the playoffs or not. A Cincinnati loss would hand the Astros' their second straight division title—regardless of whether or not they beat the Dodgers. Seaver took the mound for the Reds and endured a shaky first inning, with a single, a stolen base, and a single to put runners on first and third. Seaver induced a double play, but the run scored. Foster had Seaver's back, though. In the bottom of the first, Collins walked and Griffey singled to lead off the game. An out later, Foster crushed his 22nd and final home run of the season to deep left field. Those three runs were the only runs notched by Cincinnati against Rick Mahler, who allowed nine hits and a base runner in all but one of the seven innings he appeared in yet yielded just three runs.

Hume replaced Seaver to start the eighth and allowed back-to-back singles, putting runners at first and third. The next batter was the formidable Dale Murphy. Murphy lined out, but the go-ahead run scored on an error by Oester at second base. The Reds mounted a final threat in the eighth when Bench came to the plate with runners at first and second and one out. Although he had been the living manifestation of clutch so many times in the past, Bench could not come through on this occasion, flying out to center field. Knight struck out to end the inning, and Cincinnati went down in order in the ninth, losing 4-3. Even though the Dodgers once again topped the Astros, Houston had repeated as NL West champs.

Cincinnati won its 1981 finale 3-0 over Atlanta behind a complete-game one-hitter from Soto. The Reds had finished the second half 31-21, a game and a half behind Houston. The team's cumulative record was 66-42, the best in the majors. Nonetheless, the split-season format meant the league's top team would be watching postseason baseball from their couches instead of hosting games at Riverfront. The fact that Cincinnati lost out in part because they played two fewer games than the 110 played by Los Angeles and Houston was another laughable addendum to the season. The Reds were not alone in justifiably griping about that aspect of MLB's playoff calculus.

At the Reds' last game against the Braves, the Riverfront announcer introduced the players as if they were appearing in a playoff game. The club then unfurled a pennant mocking the split-season format. It read *Baseball's Best Record 1981*. After the game, Reds' manager McNamara was glum: "If I wasn't a grown man, I think I would cry on a curb or a park bench or somewhere. I don't know how to explain it or how to explain myself—still waters run deep—I'll never forget this."

> "We always act in the best interests of baseball and its fans."

BOWIE KUHN
MLB COMMISSIONER

19
MLB Defends the Split Season

THURSDAY, OCTOBER 8

GREBEY WAS BACK ON THE STAND as MLB presented its defense. He looked weary. He had met briefly with Dowd the night before at the LeVeque, and Dowd had reminded him of their preparation earlier in the week. "Ray, just answer my questions. Don't try to guess where I am going, like you did today with Wright. This will be straightforward, nothing you can't answer. Nothing you need to study. Most importantly, get a good night's sleep."

Grebey tried to follow Dowd's advice, but sleep eluded him. Grebey spent three hours reviewing his notes from the contract negotiations that had taken place during the summer, and he pondered how he might convince the judge of the good reasons for a split season. He got a lousy night's sleep, made lousier by knowing Dowd and Kuhn were pissed at him about his testimony earlier that day. Dowd had assured Grebey that Wright had not made a real case against the split-season structure, but he emphasized that Judge Jackson wanted—needed—to hear a defense that would justify denying the plaintiffs' request.

Dowd was brief in questioning Grebey. Dowd knew there was one witness Judge Jackson really wanted to hear from: Kuhn. Dowd spent his time reviewing Grebey's career by asking easy questions Grebey could answer without hesitation. He sought to counteract the defensiveness Grebey had displayed toward Miller the previous day. As he prepared to conclude, he zeroed in on the primary point he wanted the judge to take hold of.

"Mr. Grebey, was there any provision in the negotiated agreement that limited the commissioner's discretion in designing the second half of the season or the postseason?"

Grebey replied emphatically, "None. As Mr. Miller admitted earlier, we were free to structure the rest of the season as we saw fit. We wanted to keep the interests of the fans in mind, first and foremost."

"Thank you. No further questions."

Jackson perked up. He expected Dowd to waste more time in questioning Grebey. He turned to Wright: "Any further questions from the plaintiffs?"

"No, Your Honor."

"Okay, then. Mr. Dowd, any more witnesses?"

"Yes," replied Dowd. "We call Bowie Kuhn."

Kuhn, seated awkwardly at the counsel table, rose and proceeded to the witness chair. He was a 6-foot-5, bulky man pushing 250 pounds. Kuhn dressed as many male lawyers did: a dark blue suit, a white button-down shirt, and a yellow tie. He wore wire-rim glasses and offered a pleasant smile as he glanced at Judge Jackson. Kuhn looked comfortable in the chair, just as he did when he conducted meetings with team owners or press conferences with the media. He had demonstrated his skill in handling—or dodging—difficult questions from both the owners and the press in the face of frequent controversies during his reign as commissioner. To many baseball fans, Kuhn was the face and the voice of the owners, though he claimed to be impartial.

> Bowie Kent Kuhn was born in Takoma Park, Maryland, in 1926. His father, a German immigrant, was a fuel company executive. At the age of 15, Kuhn got a job working the scoreboard at Washington, D.C.'s Griffith Stadium for a dollar a day during Senators' games. He studied economics at Princeton University before obtaining his law degree from the University of Virginia in 1950. After law school, Kuhn accepted a position at a New York City law firm that represented the National League. For much of the next 18 years, he toiled on many baseball matters. His most noteworthy accomplishment during that period was successfully representing the league when the city of Milwaukee sued it after the Braves moved to Atlanta following the 1965 season.
>
> When the owners forced out Commissioner William Eckert in 1968, Kuhn was an obvious choice to become the fifth commissioner of baseball in January 1969. The position had no stated term, so there was job security only as long as most owners were happy with his performance. In many ways, it was amazing that by the time of the 1981 strike, he had managed to survive 12 years given MLB's tumultuous relationship with the Players Association. Kuhn had earned the loyalty of many owners because of his early moves to strengthen their bottom line. During the first decade of his tenure, there was unprecedented growth in the game. Between 1969 (when Kuhn was hired) and 1980, the league's total attendance tripled and annual television revenue increased by more than $10 million. Kuhn's tenure, which was marked by battles over free agency and players' drug use, ended in 1984.

Dowd began his questioning by asking Kuhn to explain MLB's expansion from 20 to 24 teams in the late 1960s, with new franchises awarded to Montreal, Seattle, San Diego, and Kansas City. As Kuhn noted, while expansion was exciting for fans and lucrative for the new team owners, there were drawbacks too. It was hard enough selling tickets to fans when their teams were in 9th or 10th place in either league, but now 11th or 12th place? Also, although pennant races late in the season meant a bump in ticket sales for the contending teams, increasing the number of teams meant there were more teams in the also-ran category.

Kuhn testified that while he had always remained committed to upholding baseball's hallowed traditions, as a new commissioner he came to believe that some restructuring was needed within Major League Baseball. So in 1969, he created two six-team divisions (East and West) in each league. In order to reach the World Series, the top finishers in each league's two divisions had to play each other first. (What Kuhn failed to mention was that under this structure, sixth place in a division amounted to last place, but finishing sixth certainly sounded better than 11th or 12th!) He conceded that this change was received as a major shake-up among baseball's faithful fans, because it was now possible that the team with the best record in each league might not make it to the World Series.

Judge Jackson interrupted Kuhn before he went further. "So did that happen? Did teams get to the World Series without having the best record in their league?"

Kuhn replied, "Not for the first three years under the new structure, but it happened in 1972 when the Reds had one less win than the Pittsburgh Pirates but beat them in the league playoffs and advanced to the World Series." The commissioner went on to boast that MLB prospered under the revised playoff structure despite team owners sharing more revenue with players than they had before. Kuhn unabashedly told Judge Jackson that under his tenure, attendance increased by 60 percent, teams' gross revenues rose by 144 percent, television revenues soared by 355 percent, and the top sale price of a club rose from $10 million to $21 million.

Kuhn punctuated his comments with the observation that the Reds fans complaining about the playoff format were ignoring history. Raising his voice, he noted, "There was no lawsuit in 1972 when Cincinnati benefitted by making it to the playoffs despite not finishing first in their league!"

Jackson suddenly interrupted. "That seems entirely irrelevant to our situation today. When you introduced the divisional structure and altered the playoff format in 1969, those changes were announced *before* the season. Do you really think the 1969 realignment justifies your split-season scheme this year?"

Kuhn hesitated and took a sip of water from the paper cup on the witness stand. "No, Your Honor. I am just explaining that we always act in the best interests of baseball and its fans. Occasionally, those decisions benefit some teams and their fans and hurt others. But everyone understands that we try to do what is best for baseball overall."

Jackson seemed unimpressed. "You mentioned 1972. According to my research, in 1973, the New York Mets made it to the World Series but had 17 fewer wins than Cincinnati during the season and fewer wins than Los Angeles and San Francisco. And Oakland won the World Series that year with only the third best record in baseball. I really don't understand your position, including why any work stoppage was needed this year given that the owners are doing so well under your leadership."

Dowd frowned. This was the first time Jackson had interjected himself in the trial with a display of historical baseball knowledge. Dowd knew history was on the fans' side because this season was such an aberration.

He also knew many owners thought the carnage of the strike would ultimately work to their advantage.

Before Kuhn could respond, Jackson continued. "Correct me if I'm wrong, but since then there have been only four World Series between teams with the best records in their leagues, right? Is that fact good or bad for your position in this case?"

Kuhn was not sure what to say. He could see the trap being set by Jackson and knew he had to tread carefully. "Neither," he replied. "The only point I am making is that the clubs have altered the rules in the past, and the best record did not guarantee a World Series appearance for the last 12 years. And no one filed a lawsuit!"

Jackson leaned in. "Well, but isn't the real point pretty obvious? Before this year, the teams with the best record in their division always made the playoffs and were guaranteed a chance to compete in the postseason, right?"

Kuhn did not know how to respond, and the question hung in the air like a lazy fly ball.

Jackson continued. "Mr. Kuhn, I read a quote from you in *The New York Times* several years ago. You stated then that, '[The commissioner] should use his powers fearlessly to protect the integrity of the game. The critics will call him self-righteous and moralistic. Have courage. Ignore them.' Jackson paused, then asked "Doesn't the split-season playoff format compromise the integrity of the game?"

Kuhn turned and looked directly at Judge Jackson: "Sir, I have always acted with integrity. No one forced me to design the split-season playoff. I believed, and still do, that we preserved the integrity of the game because more consequential games were played after the strike by virtue of more teams being in the hunt. And the union certainly never objected!" Kuhn seemed agitated that the judge was questioning him at all, much less asking tough questions.

Replied Jackson, "But did the union sign off on the split season? I thought they were not even consulted."

This question hit a nerve, as Kuhn took it to mean he was being accused of acting without integrity and that the judge was viewing the union as being blameless. Kuhn knew he needed to address the judge's questions directly for fear of losing his credibility; instead, he lost his cool:

> Your Honor, Mr. Miller's foolhardy idea to call a strike cost the players nearly $30 million. Players have the spirit of thoroughbreds and were led by Miller as a trusting light brigade into the valley of death. You ask about integrity? Mr. Miller turned insincerity into an art form. Guided by an ego that was the North Star of his life, he followed it wherever it led. Fortunately for the players, the path that star took sometimes coincided with the path of their own destiny. This year, it did not. He has left a legacy of hatred and bitterness between the clubs and the players that will effectively destroy labor relations in baseball for years to come. He was not the only cause of the strike, but he was the preponderant one. Miller had planned the strike for almost 15 years. There was not a chance in hell I would have asked his permission to have a split season, because any objection from him could have threatened the whole season!

Jackson didn't react to Kuhn's monologue. "Okay. Mr. Dowd, I'm sorry to have interrupted your questioning. You may continue."

Dowd was not sure what to ask. He had planned to follow their script that would shed light on the difficult choices every commissioner has to make, but he felt he needed to have Kuhn answer the judge's question more directly. "Mr. Kuhn," he said, "please tell Judge Jackson why you ultimately decided to move forward with the split-season playoffs."

Kuhn answered:

> It's really quite simple. Because of the strike, both the players and owners had lost money. My charge was to find a way to recoup some of the lost revenue after the strike ended. We know that the determinants of revenue in the four major North American sports leagues are on-field success through winning and playoff participation, market size as measured by population, and the age of the facility where a team competes. We could not influence the latter two, but we could increase the likelihood of on-field success by having every team remain in playoff contention when play resumed. The intent has always been to have an expanded playoff only for this season—one that has been irregular in a number of ways. Our idea—and I think it's the right one—was that having more teams in contention would increase revenue for all parties. The alternative was a scenario where most teams had no reasonable chance to make the playoffs and therefore no way to sustain fan interest.

Dowd followed up. "Were you intending to hurt the teams that had the best records at the time?"

"Of course not," replied Kuhn. "They all had a chance to win the second half, and the teams that performed the best in the second half made the playoffs. You'll notice that the Reds and Cardinals owners are not here. They knew the rules going into the second half of the season, and they understood my logic. Our approach serves the long-term interests of the game and is not only about this season."

Jackson interrupted again from his perch to the right of Kuhn. "But the Reds and Cardinals voted against the split-season concept, right?"

"Yes," answered Kuhn. "But once the majority of owners voted, both clubs respected the decision. They are satisfied that we made the right decision for the sport even though it hurt their clubs."

Dowd wanted to finish on that point. "Mr. Kuhn, you are telling us that the Reds' owners are supportive of your decision to split the season?"

"Absolutely," Kuhn insisted.

Added Dowd, "Have they or any other club complained to you about the playoff structure?"

"No," stated Kuhn.

Dowd faced Jackson. "Nothing further, Your Honor."

Jackson gazed at Wright: "Any questions?"

Wright leaned over, winked again at the boys, and slowly stepped to the left side of the counsel table. "We have just one question." *The judge had asked most of our questions for us,* he thought to himself.

Wright actually asked two questions, but allowed Kuhn only one answer. "Mr. Kuhn, isn't Marvin Miller the villain to most of the owners because he is the most effective union organizer since John L. Lewis organized the mine workers and steelworkers a half century ago? Without him, baseball would still be as it always was before—players largely under the control of the owners and devoid of negotiating leverage. To MLB, Miller caused Armageddon with his demands for players to be treated like high-priced employees who should have the right to play for the highest bidder. Isn't that all true, and shouldn't your loyalty be to both the owners and the players?"

With his jaw set, Kuhn looked directly at Wright and responded, "I can't dispute your statements about Mr. Miller if all you are looking at are the gains made by the players. I am tasked with taking both sides into consideration in my role as commissioner, and I believe the union went too far. I acted to save the game."

Wright responded: "No further questions."

Jackson was pleased that Wright concluded his questions. But the judge had a final question for Kuhn. "Commissioner, is it practical to hold all of the playoffs that resulted from your split season decision—the four division series, the two league championships, and the World Series—if we have a decision on this matter tomorrow?"

Kuhn leaned forward, not sure where Jackson was going. "Frankly, with travel, perhaps some time to prepare the players again, and the potential for weather delays, it will be hard to conclude before November, but that is our desire. We'll be nimble enough to provide what the fans deserve."

It was late in the afternoon, and Jackson wanted to wrap things up. "No more witnesses, Mr. Dowd?"

Dowd rose and said, "No further witnesses, Your Honor. That concludes our defense. We rest."

"Very well," said Jackson. The matter is submitted and the record is closed. Given the urgency of the situation, I will announce my decision promptly at 9:00 a.m. tomorrow. See you then."

George Grande immediately filed a report for *SportsCenter* outside the courtroom. "What an afternoon in Columbus, Ohio! The commissioner of baseball was under a microscope. Baseball fans, we will hear in the morning whether the MLB playoffs will get underway as planned or if the judge has other ideas. At this point, it seems like a toss-up. We will have extensive coverage of Bowie Kuhn's testimony and more coverage of this extraordinary lawsuit at 6:00 p.m."

Back in his chambers, Jackson was troubled by the weight of his impending decision. He was unpersuaded by the plaintiffs' legal arguments, but Jackson was bothered by the injustice of MLB's decision, as well as the commissioner's arrogance. *The owners seem to think they can play by their own rules,* he thought. As is customary before judges issue rulings, he summoned his three law clerks: Josephine Wood, Del Ott, and Gillian Hodges.

The jurist and his would-be lawyers sat around a small coffee table, Jackson in a wingback chair and the law clerks on a long couch facing him. Jackson slid off his shoes, as he was prone to do. Off to the side, Archibald Graham slouched in an uncomfortable wishbone chair that he carried in from his adjoining office. The five discussed the merits of each party's arguments, but mostly they focused on the courtroom having been the focus of the nation's attention. They doubted that they would see the likes of it again.

Wood exclaimed, "Jesus, who knew how big this would be when Chick brought in the complaint and the TRO motion on Friday afternoon?" Ott and Hodges laughed, but Jackson was all business.

After taking 30 more minutes to collect his thoughts, Jackson stood up and addressed the clerks. "I want the three of you to find me some legal precedent from baseball history, and let's get this done by midnight! You know what I want."

Indeed, the law clerks knew precisely what the judge wanted to announce the next day.

The Reds weren't the only team unfairly eliminated by MLB's asinine split season.

20

More Than Just a Big Red Mess

IN THE NATIONAL LEAGUE EAST, defending champion Philadelphia faded following its first-half finish as the division leader. In the Phillies' stead rose St. Louis and Montreal, the latter seeking its first playoff berth since its inaugural season in 1969, the same year baseball expanded its postseason from two to four teams. The Expos clinched the NL East's second-half championship with its play down the stretch; Montreal won 11 of its final 15 games to finish 30-23, a half-game ahead of St. Louis (29-23).

FINAL NL WEST SECOND-HALF STANDINGS					
Team	Wins	Losses	Ties	W/L %	Games Back
Houston Astros	33	20	0	.623	—
Cincinnati Reds	31	21	0	.596	1.5
San Francisco Giants	29	23	0	.558	3.5
Los Angeles Dodgers	27	26	0	.509	6.0
Atlanta Braves	25	27	0	.481	7.5
San Diego Padres	18	36	0	.333	15.5

FINAL NL EAST SECOND-HALF STANDINGS

Team	Wins	Losses	Ties	W/L %	Games Back
Montreal Expos	30	23	0	.566	—
St. Louis Cardinals	29	23	0	.558	0.5
Philadelphia Phillies	25	27	0	.481	4.5
New York Mets	24	28	1	.462	5.5
Chicago Cubs	23	28	1	.451	6.0
Pittsburgh Pirates	21	33	0	.389	9.5

CUMULATIVE NL WEST STANDINGS (Playoff teams in bold)

Team	W	L	Ties	W/L %	Games Back	Games Played
Cincinnati Reds	66	42	0	.611	—	108
Los Angeles Dodgers	63	47	0	.573	4.0	110
Houston Astros	61	49	0	.555	6.0	110
San Francisco Giants	56	55	0	505	11.5	111
Atlanta Braves	50	56	1	.472	15.0	107
San Diego Padres	41	69	0	.373	26.0	110

CUMULATIVE NL EAST STANDINGS (Playoff teams in bold)

Team	W	L	Ties	W/L %	Games Back	Games Played
St. Louis Cardinals	59	43	1	.578	—	103
Montreal Expos	60	48	0	.556	2.0	108
Philadelphia Phillies	59	48	0	.551	2.5	107
Pittsburgh Pirates	46	56	1	.451	13.0	103
New York Mets	41	62	2	.398	18.5	105
Chicago Cubs	38	65	3	.369	21.5	106

Much like the Reds, the Cardinals were scammed out of a playoff spot. St. Louis won the NL East by two games over the entire season—despite playing five fewer games than Montreal and four fewer than Philadelphia. In the second half, Montreal and Houston "won" their second-half titles, but neither would have prevailed in their division had the entire season been taken into consideration. The Expos would have been close at two games back in second place in the NL East, but Houston would have placed third in the NL West, six games back.

The two teams that had been guaranteed a spot in August, Philadelphia and Los Angeles, both played so poorly in the last eight weeks of the season that they would have been eliminated from World Series contention had the rules at the start of the season been honored. The Phillies finished third in the NL East over the entire season, and the Dodgers were second in the NL West, four games behind the Reds.

The American League standings weren't quite as farcical, but they were close. The Milwaukee Brewers (31-22) claimed the second-half American League East crown, five games ahead of the Yankees, who had won the division's first half. In the AL West, Kansas City, which finished 10 games under .500 (20-30) in the first half, won the second-half title with a record of 30-23, one game ahead of first-half champion Oakland.

FINAL AL WEST SECOND-HALF STANDINGS

Team	Wins	Losses	Ties	W/L %	Games Back
Kansas City Royals	30	23	0	.566	—
Oakland Athletics	27	22	0	.551	1.0
Texas Rangers	24	26	0	.480	4.5
Minnesota Twins	24	29	0	.453	6.0
Seattle Mariners	23	29	0	.442	6.5
Chicago White Sox	23	30	0	.434	7.0
California Angels	20	30	0	.400	8.5

FINAL AL EAST SECOND-HALF STANDINGS

Team	Wins	Losses	Ties	W/L %	Games Back
Milwaukee Brewers	31	22	0	.585	—
Boston Red Sox	29	23	0	.558	1.5
Detroit Tigers	29	23	0	.558	1.5
Baltimore Orioles	28	23	0	.549	2.0
Cleveland Indians	26	27	0	.491	5.0
New York Yankees	25	26	0	.490	5.0
Toronto Blue Jays	21	27	0	.438	7.5

CUMULATIVE AL WEST STANDINGS (Playoff teams in bold)

Team	W	L	Ties	W/L %	Games Back	Games Played
Oakland Athletics	64	45	0	.587	—	109
Texas Rangers	57	48	0	.543	5.0	105
Chicago White Sox	54	52	0	.509	8.5	106
Kansas City Royals	50	53	0	.485	11.0	103
California Angels	51	59	0	.464	13.5	110
Seattle Mariners	44	65	1	.404	20.0	110
Minnesota Twins	41	68	1	.376	23.0	110

CUMULATIVE AL EAST STANDINGS (Playoff teams in bold)

Team	W	L	Ties	W/L %	Games Back	Games Played
Milwaukee Brewers	62	47	0	.569	—	109
Baltimore Orioles	59	46	0	.562	1.0	105
New York Yankees	59	48	0	.551	2.0	107
Detroit Tigers	60	49	0	.550	2.0	109
Boston Red Sox	59	49	0	.546	2.5	108
Cleveland Indians	52	51	0	.505	7.0	103
Toronto Blue Jays	37	69	0	.349	23.5	106

Though both Milwaukee's and Oakland's entry into the playoffs was (mostly) legitimate, there were plenty of injustices to go around. The Brewers and the Athletics owned the best records in the AL West and East, respectively, over the entirety of the season. However, Milwaukee profited from playing four more games than Baltimore. The Yankees qualified for the postseason because of their first-half finish despite placing third in the overall AL East standings and playing two more games than Baltimore, the squad that was second in the season-long standings.

The AL West was a bit of a quagmire, too—again, except for Oakland, which cleared second-place Texas by five games. (The Athletics did play four more games than the Rangers, though.) The great injustice was the inclusion of Kansas City in the postseason. The Royals had won the West's second half by a game over the Athletics, but Kansas City also played one more game than the A's in the second half. But even more egregious was Kansas City's overall record of 50-53, meaning the fourth-best team in the AL West's cumulative standings would be playing in October. Even Kansas City's Hall of Fame third baseman, George Brett, admitted, "This whole year has been a joke."

The complete failure of the split-season format and the discrepancy in games played reinforced the fact that Kuhn's plan was a travesty, and it made a mockery of the postseason. Fans and baseball purists were not happy with MLB's decision, and most baseball columnists thought the arrangement was ludicrous.

Literary critic and self-proclaimed baseball buff Jonathan Yardley declared that "the owners are a group of men whose stupidity is exceeded by their avarice." Thomas Boswell, the widely respected baseball writer for *The Washington Post*, also weighed in: "Every time we look at the split season standings, the nonsense of a mini playoff, the decimated statistics of an asterisk season, we [will be] reminded of baseball's ugliest episode."

After this forgettable decision, fans' interest declined in the last two months of the 1981 season as indicated by attendance dropping measurably despite Kuhn's prediction to the contrary. To many, Kuhn was the villain because of the wrongheaded assumptions that informed his playoff decree.

The Reds' manager, McNamara, was still hot about being left out: "It's been a mess, that's what it's been. To get cheated out of it by somebody's lamebrain idea is even worse." In contrast, even though St. Louis lost the second half by virtue of playing one less game than Montreal, the Cardinals' manager, Whitey Herzog, shrugged it all off. On the chartered jet from Pittsburgh after their season finale, he joked that the Cardinals would work out that night and then head to Hawaii for the start of the real playoffs against the Reds. The Reds' team publicist, Jim Ferguson, jokingly responded that the series would begin in Evansville, Indiana, a "neutral site." But to die-hard Reds fans, it was hard to find any humor in the situation. It was way too soon for joking.

True to his word, Dick Wagner adopted a "what's-done-is-done" attitude and moved on. Marvin Miller is the culprit, not MLB, he said. Once the season ended, he could be found in his office at Riverfront Stadium consulting with George Yund, his labor lawyer. They were close to signing Dave Concepción—a future Hall of Famer, in Wagner's estimation—to the largest contract in club history. He knew he needed to keep Concepción to appease fans who were upset with the Reds' exclusion from the postseason.

But unlike Wagner and Herzog, *St. Louis Post-Dispatch* sports editor Bob Broeg was not over it. In his mind, the Cardinals' third-best record in baseball afforded them little more than the chance to "contemplate their navels" in the off-season.

"Thus, the question before this Court is whether Mr. Kuhn acted in the best interests of the game and for the good of the game in declaring a split season."

JOSEPH JACKSON
FEDERAL JUDGE

21

The Decision

FRIDAY, OCTOBER 9

MARCONI BOULEVARD WAS BUSTLING early in the morning. The morning commute from Columbus's western suburbs rivaled the traffic snarl from the 1977 blizzard that hit the capital city. By 8:30, courthouse personnel placed a large sign in front of the main entrance: "At Capacity. No Entry Other Than Staff and Counsel." The sign had never been used before.

On the second floor, the courtroom gallery was packed, but it was eerily quiet as everyone awaited Judge Jackson's arrival. Mixed in with media representatives and MLB executives were dozens of fans, most of whom had been wearing hats adorned with the Reds logo before taking their place in the gallery. Bill O'Conner, who had corralled his friends to come earlier in the week, returned again along with the same friends. They looked exhausted, perhaps because they had crashed O'Conner's apartment the night before and partied until after midnight. In Cincinnati, 100 miles to the south, hundreds of fans had camped out at Riverfront Stadium overnight hoping that playoff tickets would go on sale.

Far, Queen, and Smack arrived with Wright's legal team shortly before

9:00, followed by the column of MLB lawyers and staff members. After Bowie Kuhn pulled up the rear, everyone took a seat. No pleasantries were exchanged between the warring sides.

Archibald Graham, the bailiff, entered from the side of the courtroom, prompting the spectators to rise in unison. "Hear ye, hear ye, this honorable court for the Southern District of Ohio is now in session. All persons having business before the court, draw attention, and ye shall be heard. God save the United States and this honorable court."

Judge Jackson entered through the same door and ascended hurriedly to his bench. "Please be seated." He paused, glancing at the audience. Jackson began:

> Good morning. The court has reviewed the entire record in this matter and has reached a decision that will be entered formally on the docket after it is typed and finalized later this morning. We spent the bulk of the evening and early this morning writing our order knowing the urgency of the matter for the parties and other interested members of the public. For now, I will read the pertinent portions of my order. For almost 60 years, the federal courts have treated professional baseball as a whole and Major League Baseball in particular differently than other businesses on the legal theory that baseball is a sport, not a matter of interstate commerce. Therefore, in 1922, the United States Supreme Court exempted baseball from antitrust laws on that very basis in *Federal Baseball League v. National League.*

Dowd looked nervously at Kuhn. *This doesn't sound like a good start.* The boys, and the fans in the gallery, were not sure where the judge was headed. Wright nodded at the boys as he fixed his gaze on the judge.

Jackson continued:

Around the same time, MLB decided to appoint a commissioner to oversee baseball operations and ensure that competition was fair to all teams, but also to restore public trust in baseball in the aftermath of the 1919 Black Sox scandal. Federal judge Kenesaw Mountain Landis was installed as the first commissioner, and he was assured by team owners that his office would have nearly unlimited authority to act in the best interests of baseball.

Even after all the players who were implicated in the Black Sox scandal had been acquitted in court by a jury, Judge Landis refused to reinstate them because of the message that would be sent to the public. He denied the eight players the chance to play professional baseball at any level on the grounds that he had the authority to act in the best interest of a sport exempted from antitrust laws.

Judge Kenesaw Mountain Landis once explained his thinking about upholding the propriety of baseball as follows: "Baseball is something more than a game to an American boy; it is his training field for life work. Destroy his faith in its squareness and honesty and you have destroyed something more; you have planted suspicion of all things in his heart."

Judge Jackson continued with his monologue about Commissioner Landis:

> During his nearly 25-year tenure, the courts permitted him to deal harshly with players who threw games, consorted with gamblers, or engaged in actions that he felt tarnished the image of the game. Among the players he banned were New York Giants players Phil Douglas and Jimmy O'Connell and Philadelphia Phillies pitcher Gene Paulette. He also tossed Giants coach Cozy Dolan out of baseball for offering a bribe and banned Phillies owner William D.

Cox for betting on his own team. Landis's power was so unchecked that he banned Giants center fielder Benny Kauff even though Kauff was acquitted of involvement in a car theft ring. Landis was convinced Kauff was guilty and argued that players of undesirable reputation and character had no place in baseball.

As baseball fans know, Judge Landis is credited with having restored the American people's trust in the integrity of Major League Baseball. Subsequent commissioners have also been granted almost unlimited latitude to act in the best interests of baseball. But the power is not entirely unlimited.

Following Judge Landis's lead, Commissioner Kuhn has suspended numerous players for involvement with drugs and gambling, and he has taken a strong stance against any activity that he did not perceive to be "in the best interests of baseball." For example, in 1970, he suspended star Detroit Tigers pitcher Denny McLain for three months due to McLain's involvement in a bookmaking operation, and he later suspended McLain for the rest of the season for carrying a gun. He barred former player Willie Mays from working in baseball just two years ago due to his involvement in casino promotions. Each of these actions deprived these men the opportunity to earn substantial income, and the courts were not going to interfere.

Mr. Kuhn has been given similar authority over the owners. When Mr. Finley attempted to sell several players to the Boston Red Sox and New York Yankees in return for $3.5 million, the commissioner blocked the deals on the grounds that they would be bad for the game.

All of this is premised on what MLB told the Supreme Court in 1973 in *Curt Flood v. Kuhn*. The Supreme Court denied Mr. Flood's request for free agency, accepting MLB's argument that Commissioner Kuhn acted the way he did for the good of the game.

> Indeed, Mr. Kuhn testified yesterday that he declared the split season because he thinks he was acting in the best interests of baseball and its fans. Thus, the question before this Court is whether Mr. Kuhn acted in the best interests of the game and for the good of the game in declaring a split season.

Jackson paused and looked up from his prepared remarks. Jackson's drawn expression made him look like an undertaker. But was he conducting a funeral for the fans or for Commissioner Kuhn? All of a sudden, it seemed that both sides had a chance—Judge Jackson was focusing on whether the split season was in the best interests of baseball, yet there was no discernible means for adjudicating that. Everyone was on edge. Kuhn was particularly anxious because he, rather than the owners, was the focal point of the judge's analysis. It did not take long for the jurist to end the suspense:

> The court has determined that Major League Baseball, for much of this century, has promised fans in general and season ticket holders in particular that all regular season games figure into playoff eligibility. The ticket-buying public and people listening to or watching broadcasts have been told that the World Series marks the culmination of the best teams' season-long performance. Granted, Major League Baseball expanded the field in 1969 from what it had encompassed previously, but the basic premise was still intact: all games over an entire season determined the participants of the league playoffs leading up to the World Series.
>
> On a motion like this, I sit in equity. The World Series will take place, this year only, in the same manner that it did prior to 1969. This late in October makes it impractical to have a full round of playoffs and then a World Series. Weather is simply too unpredictable and MLB has an interest in avoiding postseason baseball in November.

Accordingly, I hereby order that a World Series championship be held as soon as practical between the two teams with the best records in baseball over the entire season—the Cincinnati Reds from the National League and the Oakland Athletics from the American League.

The World Series will not begin before October 16 to allow the Reds time to reconvene and for the Athletics organization to make necessary preparations. In addition to getting their players ready to play in the Series, Oakland has to prepare the venue to host the first two games. Because of this delay, there is no rationale in holding the Division Series or League Championship Series. MLB will work in good faith with the Players Association to determine the fine details of the logistics involved.

An ovation and a small amount of smuggled-in confetti arose from the gallery, and this time Jackson allowed the disturbances to go unabated for several seconds before banging his gavel. O'Conner—the dental student—smiled broadly as he exchanged high fives with his buddies, Finley, Kneflin, Sharbell, and Murphy. In his best stage whisper, O'Conner leaned over and said, "Gentlemen, how long will it take to drive to Oakland?"

The plaintiffs bowed their heads as if in prayer, mostly out of a sense of disbelief that they had won. Wright had instructed them not to show any reaction regardless of the ruling. Wright and his team gathered their papers as if it were just another day in court. Kuhn looked like he had just seen the ghost of Shoeless Joe Jackson. Dowd slowly packed his bags without looking at his client. The media rushed out the rear gallery door, another breach of courtroom etiquette that Jackson tolerated. He knew it was no use to berate anyone now that the case was over.

When calm descended on the room, Jackson looked squarely at Dowd and Kuhn. "Gentlemen, I understand you disagree with my decision, but I believe it is in the best interests of baseball and its fans. I don't think you'll have trouble selling tickets. Who knows? This may turn out to be the most watched World Series of all time. I hope so, and I wish you the best."

Jackson abruptly rose from his chair, and exited out the side door followed by his courtroom staff and law clerks.

ESPN, CNN, and the major television networks broke into regular programming with "Breaking News" explaining the court's ruling. Most members of the media were describing the plaintiffs' victory as the greatest upset in sports history.

An hour after the ruling, a dejected Dowd and Kuhn met with a respectfully cheerful Miller at Hotel LeVeque. MLB would respect Jackson's decision—an appeal was impractical if they wanted to make any money off the 1981 postseason—but the World Series needed to start as soon as possible to increase their odds of palatable fall weather in Cincinnati and Oakland. The meeting lasted for 90 minutes, and shortly thereafter Kuhn issued a press release stating that the World Series would begin on Saturday, October 17, in Oakland. A week, he explained, was necessary to allow the two teams to prepare, particularly since many of the Reds had scattered across the country. And, of course, Kuhn reiterated that his main concern was for the fans and the integrity of the World Series.

Not stated was MLB's intention to hype the Series for eight days. Kuhn realized that baseball's new competitor for the title of America's Pastime— the NFL—allowed two weeks between the end of its playoffs and the Super Bowl. If the media attention helped the NFL drive ratings, he hoped the same would be true for MLB.

Then Kuhn made the most controversial decision: all games of the World Series would be broadcast on ABC in prime time! This was a break in baseball tradition, as every Fall Classic to date included some day games. His decision was widely criticized by the media as another exercise in greed—*all the kids will be sleeping by the fourth inning!*—but ABC loved the idea. Bogusz, who greenlit the proposal but allowed Kuhn to claim the idea as his own—remarked to Kuhn that having all the games at night was "a tremendous way to appease advertisers and draw a large audience."

Oakland and Cincinnati both unleashed their star power in vying to be seen as the preeminent team of the '70s.

22

Dueling Dynasties

HISTORICALLY, THE REDS' MAIN CLAIM TO FAME has been its identity as the first all-professional team, initially known as the Red Stockings. The A's also boast a long history, having ties to three cities since the club was founded in 1903 as the Philadelphia Athletics. By 1981, the Reds had played in eight World Series, winning four, but they had lost to the Athletics in a seven-game World Series in 1972, dropping a crushing Game 7 at Riverfront Stadium. Oakland had appeared in 11 World Series, winning eight. The last three triumphs had come in successive seasons in Oakland from 1972 to 1974, but prior to that, the franchise's World Series successes and failures took place when the club was based in Philadelphia. The A's played in eight World Series between 1910 and 1931, all under the "Tall Tactician," legendary manager Connie Mack, who guided the club for 50 years. (Yes, as in five decades.)

The Reds' combination of consistent winning throughout the 1970s and the sustained presence of the aforementioned Big Red Machine are why Cincinnati surpassed Oakland in the public's perception as the "team of the '70s" and as one of the best teams of all time. Oakland might beg to differ, as it reached the ALCS each season from 1971 to 1975 and owned a 3-2 advantage in World Series wins over the Reds during that span.

The A's possessed ample star power, too, with the likes of Catfish Hunter, Reggie Jackson, Rollie Fingers, and Vida Blue suiting up for the green and gold. The first three were inducted as Hall of Famers in retirement. Those four players accumulated 16 All-Star appearances, a pair of Cy Young awards, and an MVP award during their time in Oakland. But all four were gone from Oakland after 1976, compiling impressive accomplishments elsewhere.

Oakland closed out the 1970s with three straight losing seasons, including an abominable 54-108 mark in 1979. The team failed to make the postseason from 1976 to 1979. Although Oakland narrowly edged Cincinnati in World Series titles in the 1970s, the Big Red Machine secured one more division title, played in one more World Series, and triumphed in more regular season contests (953-838). Furthermore, the 1975 and 1976 Reds remain two of the most feared outfits ever assembled, with the former winning 108 regular-season games and the World Series and the latter prevailing in 102 regular-season games and seven straight playoff games in 1976, repeating as world champions. Again, casual and serious baseball fans remember the Reds as more dominant than the A's during the 1970s because of their consistently high performance, not to mention star power.

As for 1981, while Cincinnati retained players from the 1972 team—namely Bench, Concepción, and Foster, who were keen on avenging the Big Red Machine's second World Series loss—Oakland was a completely new group. Not one player from the 1972 squad was still around. Hunter departed after the 1974 season, followed in successive seasons by Jackson (1975), Fingers (1976), and Blue (1977).

After bottoming out in 1979, Oakland won nearly 30 more games in

1980, finishing 83-79 under the stewardship of fiery first-year manager Billy Martin. The turnaround was paced by a speedy 21-year-old outfielder, Rickey Henderson, who had debuted the year before. He quickly blossomed into a star in 1980, racking up an incredible 8.8 WAR in the first of his 10 All-Star seasons. Henderson hit .303, reached base in 42 percent of his plate appearances, and stole 100 bases. Henderson's fellow starting outfielders, Dwayne Murphy (6.9 WAR, and the Gold Glove winner in center field) and Tony Armas (5.9 WAR, 35 home runs, 109 RBI), were the other standout position players. On the mound, Mike Norris (22 wins, 2.53 ERA, second in AL Cy Young); Rick Langford (19 wins, 3.26 ERA, MLB-best 28 complete games); and Matt Keough (16 wins, 2.92 ERA) led a staff that ranked first in the American League in ERA. With all of them still in their 20s—most in their mid-20s—Oakland's foundation was set for another run of excellence.

The A's continued their ascent in 1981, beginning the season by terminating all opponents. Oakland began the year with a then-AL record 11 consecutive victories, plating 58 runs and allowing just 13. Martin's outfit finished April with an 18-3 record, already up 4.5 games in the AL West. It's worth noting that Oakland's April dominance came against California, Minnesota, and Seattle, squads that finished the season with three of the AL's four worst records. Minnesota (41-68) and Seattle (44-65) were particularly terrible.

Nevertheless, Oakland's opening month was magnificent, particularly on the pitching side. Norris won all five of his starts, notching a 2.14 ERA in the process. Keough was even better, winning his four starts and limiting the opposition to a 1.00 ERA. For the month, the A's never allowed more than four runs in a game and yielded just 41 runs in 21 games. The starting staff of Norris, Keough, Langford, Steve McCatty and Brian Kingman were featured on the April 27, 1981, cover of *Sports Illustrated*.

A stone-cold case of regression to the mean hit Oakland in May, however. An eight-game losing streak in the middle of the month to stronger teams (Milwaukee, New York, and Baltimore) gave way to a 13-17 mark in May, trimming the A's AL West advantage to a single game entering June. But Oakland rebounded before the strike halted the season, winning six of nine to claim the first-half AL West crown—and as it later turned out, a playoff berth—at 37-23, a game ahead of the Texas Rangers (33-22), who had the misfortune of playing five fewer games than the A's. (Again, the Reds weren't the only team to be screwed over by the split season.)

In the second half, Oakland played above-.500 ball in each month, going 10-9 in August, 15-12 in September, and 2-1 in October. The A's were adversely affected by the discrepancy in games played in the race for the second-half AL West title. Kansas City (30-23) edged Oakland (27-22) by a game in the standings, but played four more games than the A's. Since Oakland was already guaranteed a spot in the postseason, the inequity was water under the bridge.

At 64-45, the A's finished 1981 with the best overall record in the American League. They were five games ahead of Texas (57-48), though the Rangers played four fewer games. Individually, the clear standout was Henderson, who went from star to superstar in 1981. At age 22, Henderson led the majors in hits (135), runs (89) and stolen bases (56). He hit .319, won his first Silver Slugger and Gold Glove awards, and narrowly missed out on MVP honors, finishing just behind Fingers (319 points to 308), who was now with Milwaukee. Fingers notched a 1.08 ERA and 28 saves in 47 games.

Armas was Oakland's second-best offensive player, walloping an AL-best 22 home runs and driving in 76 runs, just two behind Baltimore's Eddie Murray for the league lead. Murphy turned in another good season, hitting 15 homers and winning his second straight Gold Glove in center field. Cliff Johnson, a journeyman who primarily served as the A's designated hitter, hit 17 homers and drove in 59 runs. (A designated hitter would not be allowed in this Series because the use of a DH alternated between even and odd years for the World Series, and this was an odd year in more ways than one.)

Again, Oakland's strength was its pitching staff, which placed second in the AL in ERA (3.30), with each of the five regular starters clocking ERAs under 4.0. The A's arms paced the league with 60 (!!!) complete games, with Langford (18), McCatty (16) and Norris (12) finishing first, second, and tied for fourth, respectively, in the AL in complete games. The 27-year-old McCatty turned in a career year, tying for the major league lead in wins (14) while pacing the AL in ERA (2.33) and shutouts (four; tied with three others). The right-hander threw 185.2 innings and finished second behind Fingers in the AL Cy Young voting. Langford (12 wins, 2.99 ERA) led the staff with 195.1 innings pitched. Norris (12 wins, 3.75 ERA) and Keough (10 wins, 3.40 ERA) also tallied double-digit wins, with the former logging 172.2 innings and the latter 140.1. The overreliance by Martin on his starters paid off in 1981, though it would have long-term consequences for the individual pitchers and the team. But for this season, the strategy worked like a charm.

The teams scramble to prepare as media interest skyrockets.

23

The Reimagined 1981 World Series

ONCE THE INK WAS DRY on Judge Jackson's order, print journalists and the media's talking heads wasted no time in scrutinizing the Oakland/Cincinnati matchup. Without a doubt, the 1981 World Series was going to feature two proud and accomplished franchises.

The A's had home field advantage due to the practice at that time of alternating home field advantage between the leagues from year to year. The A's qualified for the playoffs as winners of the first half, so they were still working out and preparing for the postseason to begin, but they thought they'd be facing the Kansas City Royals. Now they just had to focus on a different opponent, the Reds, whom they had not played during the regular season. By already knowing they would be in the playoffs, the A's had a head start on the Reds, who were scattered around the country. The only real change in their preparation was obtaining as much information as possible on the National League squad.

Oakland scoured every source—scouts, friendly officials from National League teams, video from Reds games—to determine the strengths and weaknesses of Reds pitchers, batters, and fielders. Does Ray Knight hit low and inside strikes? What pitches does Seaver rely on against right-handers? Where should we position the outfielders when Bench is at the plate? The beat went on for all 25 players on the Reds roster, gathering thousands of small pieces of information that they would have already had on any American League foe. (There was no interleague play at the time.)

Reds manager John McNamara told Dennis Janson of Cincinnati's WCPO-TV that he would get his team ready "as soon as I can get them all back to Cincinnati," but meanwhile he turned to the scouting department to begin the task of analyzing the A's. Every Reds player returned to Cincinnati by Sunday, October 11, to begin workouts, jokingly calling it "fall training." After two days of intrasquad games at Riverfront Stadium, the Reds took a charter flight to Oakland and arrived at 1:00 p.m. on October 14.

Bernie Stowe, the Reds' longtime clubhouse manager, made all the preparations for the club's trip to Oakland. Upon arrival, Stowe ushered the 25 players, coaches, and other team personnel into three buses that arrived 45 minutes later at the team hotel. Then, after the equipment and uniforms were loaded into six vans that met the plane, Stowe hopped in the lead van and headed to Oakland Coliseum. He unpacked the necessary equipment for practice—spikes, bats, balls, and gloves—so that everything was in place when the players arrived for a two-hour practice. It was their first practice since the final day of the regular season 10 days earlier.

Both teams practiced the next morning—the A's at 9:00 and the Reds at noon—with a media event set for that afternoon in front of more than 300 credentialed members of the press from around the globe. ESPN televised the press conference live, with George Grande as host. He was joined by the ABC-TV team that would call the games: Keith Jackson, Al Michaels, Howard Cosell, and Baltimore Orioles pitcher Jim Palmer.

Bowie Kuhn watched the conference with intense interest and shouted to his assistant, "Maybe all the media attention on the trial will actually help us score huge audiences!" This was, of course, his paramount concern since MLB had lost considerable TV revenue without the division series and the league championship series. Kuhn was acutely attuned to the strength of MLB's television reach during the coming World Series. Since 1963, Nielsen Media Research had provided World Series viewership data according to two measures: ratings and shares. Ratings reflect how many households watched a given program, or in the case of baseball, a game. In contrast, shares indicate the percentage of TV sets in use at a given time that were tuned to the game currently being aired.

To the delight of MLB owners, the public's interest in the World Series had increased over the years, with viewership typically growing as a Series went along. Not surprisingly, interest became particularly strong when there were potential elimination matchups in a Game 5 or Game 6, and especially so in a winner-take-all Game 7. In 1972, the last time the Reds and A's faced off, the Series averaged 32 million viewers, with 41 million people watching the climactic Game 7. In 1975, considered the best World Series of all time, the average grew to 35 million, with 51 million people tuned into Game 7 when the Big Red Machine won its first title. The next year, when the Reds swept the Yankees in four games, the Series still drew a remarkable 34 million, and the final game attracted 38 million.

The 1978 World Series (six games) attracted 44 million on average, the highest ever, and the Yankees' Series-clinching win in Game 6 hooked 54 million, the largest audience ever for a single game. All of this meant both ratings and share were high, with over half of the people watching television while games were being aired tuning into baseball's Fall Classic rather than other shows.

The TV success that MLB had come to enjoy had become a reliable revenue stream for team owners. The irony of this TV bonanza was obvious: MLB had contended that free agency would ruin the game, but the baseball-loving public was more than happy to spend their time and money on the product that MLB offered when free agency became a fact of life. The question that lingered was whether the controversial split season had soured fans enough that fan interest would drop significantly.

Tom Seaver

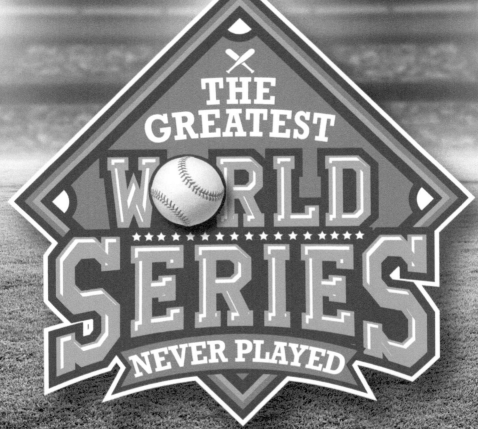

FICTION

24

Play Ball

OAKLAND, OCTOBER 17, 5:15 P.M. PDT

"Ladies and gentlemen, not in your wildest alcoholic nightmare would you have ever imagined what has transpired since the end of the regular season!" So began A's radio voice Bill King as he came on the air for Game 1 of the 1981 World Series. "I can't believe we are not playing the Royals, and I sure don't believe we have been transported by a judge's decision to the World Series. But, we'll take it. Please sit back and enjoy what undoubtedly will be the culmination of one of the wackiest seasons in the long history of Major League Baseball."

King, of course, was right. A strange season was close to a conclusion, and two teams were now vying for the 1981 world championship.

Bill King was beloved in the Bay Area, and most assumed he would someday be enshrined in Cooperstown, New York, as a Hall of Fame broadcaster. He sported a distinctive handlebar mustache and a Van Dyke beard, loved ballet and opera, and studied Russian history. He began his professional career as a member of the broadcasting team for the San Francisco Giants before

becoming the play-by-play voice of both the NFL's Oakland/Los Angeles Raiders (since 1966) and the NBA's San Francisco/Golden State Warriors (since 1962).

Prior to the 1981 season, King added the A's to his repertoire—likely the only announcer to ever take on play-by-play duties for the three major American sports at one time. When he was hired by the A's, a *San Francisco Chronicle* sportswriter reported that "King is believed to be 54. The lack of knowledge of his exact age is one of the many quirks that made King one of the great characters in Bay Area sports." (A search of Social Security records later confirmed that he was indeed 54 in 1981.) Most Oakland fans planned to *watch* the games on ABC, but they preferred to *listen* to King on KSFO 560 AM, so they turned down the volume on their televisions.

King was famous for his trademark phrase of "Holy Toledo" when he witnessed an amazing play on the field. Given his penchant for crafting unique and colorful phrases, his unorthodox introduction to Game 1 came as no surprise.

The Coliseum was jam-packed with 47,302 souls for Game 1. This solid turnout was a carryover from the odd regular season. Despite playing just 56 home games instead of 81 during a typical season, the A's set an all-time attendance record for the franchise in 1981. Enthusiasm surrounding "Billy Ball," a phrase coined to describe the aggressive style of play encouraged by second-year manager Martin—was alive and well in Oakland.

Game 1 began with A's starter Steve McCatty lighting up the capacity crowd by striking out the first three Reds batters in the top of the first. His swift start ignited a pitching duel with Reds ace and future Hall of Famer Tom Seaver. Then, after three and a half scoreless innings, Krazy George

Henderson stunned the announcers and fans.

Krazy George, who had delighted fans throughout professional sports since 1967, was Oakland's inimitable cheerleader. Now perched on the A's dugout, Krazy George suddenly engaged the fans in something he had tried at an NHL game the previous year: "the wave." Henderson motioned to one section of the stands to stand up, followed by the next, and so on. After a few false starts, the capacity crowd figured out what he was trying to do. Successive groups of spectators stood, screamed, raised their arms, and then sat back down in their seats. As a different Henderson—Rickey—was batting, the wave of fans standing in sequence traveled around the stadium.

Understandably, Seaver may have been distracted by the rhythmic cheers reverberating around the Coliseum. After setting down the first nine batters, Seaver yielded back-to-back singles to Henderson and Dwayne Murphy. With Seaver staring down Wayne Gross, Henderson and Murphy pulled off a double steal. Reds catcher Joe Nolan rushed his throw, and it sailed over Knight's head at third. Henderson scored easily and Murphy scampered into third. Billy Ball was in the house, and the A's loudspeakers played an apropos snippet from the team's fight song: "He walks off first base cool and slow, everybody in the park knows he's going to go. Billy Ball, A's baseball, Billy Ball, A's baseball, pull a double steal, do a hit and run, boy this kind of baseball sure is fun..."

After American League umpire Larry Barnett motioned for the music to stop, the wave continued, and Keith Drumright hit a sacrifice fly to make it 2-0. As the wave was reaching what seemed like its climax, Armas drilled a first-pitch fastball deep over Collins's head in right field that landed 10 rows deep into the stands. Seaver finished the inning, but the damage was done, and the Reds faced a 3-0 deficit.

McCatty cruised through the middle innings with the help of third baseman Gross, who made two remarkable snares of hard-hit balls. The A's struck again in the seventh on a two-out RBI by Dave McKay, pushing their lead to 4-0. The wave was revived intermittently, and it managed to keep the crowd energized. The Reds did not score until the ninth on a two-run, two-out homer by light-hitting second baseman Ron Oester, but A's reliever Dave Beard coaxed a soft liner off the bat of switch hitter Rafael Landestoy to shortstop Fred Stanley, sealing the victory. The A's sound system played the now familiar song at the Coliseum, Kool and the Gang's 1980 hit single, "Celebration."

BOX SCORE

CIN   000 000 002   2 6 1

OAK   000 300 10X   4 7 0

WP: McCatty (1-0), LP: Seaver (0-1), Sv: Beard (1)

Home Runs: Tony Armas (1), Ron Oester (1)

After the game, Seaver claimed he was not bothered by the fans' participation in the wave, but few reporters believed him. Reds manager McNamara was quizzed about whether the Reds anticipated the double steal. "Oh yes, we studied Billy Ball. It was just poor execution. We'll be back tomorrow night."

The Reds' trio of starters from the team that lost the Series to the A's in 1972—Bench, Concepción, and Foster—went a combined 0-11 in Game 1. Noting the A's defensive prowess on the night, Bench thought back to 1970. "I thought Brooks Robinson [the Baltimore Orioles' star third baseman who repeatedly robbed the Reds in the World Series] was playing third tonight. Gross had a helluva game." Gross was in his fifth year and had never been considered an outstanding fielder, whereas Robinson won 16 Gold Gloves at third base and had the highest fielding percentage of any third baseman when he retired in 1977. Seated by his locker after the game, Gross laughed when told about Bench comparing him to Robinson. "Sometimes, the ball just finds your glove. I had a lucky night."

Commissioner Kuhn was interviewed after the game by ABC's Al Michaels. "Commissioner, could you have asked for more?" Replied Kuhn, "That was one of the more interesting openers that we've ever had, and the energy of the crowd was amazing. I didn't know what the crowd was doing. I'm sure the fans watching at home are excited for the rest of the games." The next morning, Kuhn received the "overnights"—the first look at ratings, and he learned that more than 30 million people had tuned in. Kuhn's hype strategy was working.

It's 1972 all over again.

25

The Reds Are in a Familiar Hole

OAKLAND, OCTOBER 18, 5:15 P.M. PDT

MARTIN WAS PLEASED. Billy Ball had won Game 1. In the Game 2 pregame press conference, he opined that "the double steal changed the game." Like the Reds trying to avenge the 1972 World Series loss to the A's, Martin also had retribution on his mind. He had faced the Reds before, being on the losing end of the Reds' 1976 sweep of the Yankees. Martin held grudges, and he never forgot the embarrassment of that four-game sweep.

Martin started his managerial career with the Minnesota Twins after a decorated (and controversial) playing career. He lasted just one season in Minnesota. Martin had three-year stints with the Detroit Tigers and Texas Rangers before being hired by the Yankees in 1975. Martin was thrilled. "The only job. The Yankee job. This is the only job I ever wanted." After losing to the Reds in 1976, he guided the Yankees to a world championship in 1977, only to be fired mid-season in 1978 after criticizing Yankees' star Reggie Jackson and owner George Steinbrenner. "One's a born liar, the other's convicted." Nonetheless, he was rehired by Steinbrenner the next year only to be fired again after that season. He then was brought on by the

A's. Martin brought his fiery style to Oakland. One of his early contributions was to help outfielder Armas blossom into an exceptional player.

> **Antonio Rafael Armas Machado was born in Puerto Piritu, Venezuela, in 1953, one of 13 children. Less than 18 years later, he debuted in the minor leagues for an affiliate of the Pittsburgh Pirates. "Tony" languished for six years and concluded his Pirates career with just six at-bats. He was traded along with five others to Oakland during spring training in 1977. The A's, then in a rebuilding year, noted his defensive talents and immediately made him a starting outfielder, but injuries limited his play in 1978 and 1979. In Martin's first year, Armas avoided injury, became the A's full-time right fielder, and achieved stardom. He cracked 35 homers, batted in 109, and hit .279. He had arrived.**
>
> **After co-leading the American League in home runs in the split season of 1981 (tied with Bobby Grich, Eddie Murray, and Dwight Evans), Armas was a first-time All-Star and finished fourth in the AL MVP voting. His defense likely set him apart from the other sluggers, with one outstanding play after another in the outfield. He made only two errors and had eight assists.**

On this night, the Reds jumped out to an early 3-0 lead thanks to RBI by Foster, Joe Nolan, and Oester. The A's plated two runs in the fourth. In the fifth, Bench launched a ball to deep right field. King thought the Reds had extended their advantage. "There's a blast. Armas going back, he leaps against the padding, reaches up over the fence, but that ball is out of here!" After Armas descended back to earth, he pulled the ball out of his glove. King, the crowd, and millions watching on television were stunned. "No, it isn't! Armas has the ball! What a catch. Holy Toledo!" Bench shook his head in disbelief after rounding second base. The wave returned during the commercial break.

The A's tied the game in the next frame on a perfectly executed squeeze play by Keith Drumright, scoring Henderson, who had tripled over Griffey's head in right to lead off the frame. All McNamara could do was shake his head—Billy Ball was back. Both teams netted two runs in the seventh and headed to the final two frames knotted at five.

Gross returned to haunt the Reds to start the eighth. In a matter of seconds, he had both robbed Concepción of a sure RBI double and forced Griffey out at second with a diving stab and throw. One out later, Bench looped a double over Gross, but both he and Concepción were stranded in scoring position. Doug Bair entered in the bottom of the eighth and promptly hit Rickey Henderson, who stole second on the next pitch. After the following two batters fanned, Armas hit a towering round-tripper to the left-field bleachers. A's 7, Reds 5. Driessen doubled to lead off the ninth, and catcher Joe Nolan followed with an RBI single to left. After a visit from Martin, Bob Owchinko secured the save with a pair of routine pop-ups before striking out Dave Collins to end Game 2. Final: 7-6, A's.

Just as they had in 1972, the Reds had dropped the first two games of the World Series to the A's. The only difference was in '72, the two losses had come at Riverfront Stadium, where Cincinnati would now head with its back firmly planted against the wall. The Reds had lost with both Seaver and Soto on the mound. It was time for Bench, Concepción, Foster, and Griffey to muster their World Series magic of years past.

BOX SCORE

CIN 120 000 201 6 12 0

OAK 000 210 22X 7 12 0

WP: Langford (1-0), **LP:** Bair (0-1), **Sv:** Owchinko (1)

Home Runs: Tony Armas (2)

Back home,

the Reds seek to avoid

a dreaded 3-0 deficit.

26

The Machine Gets Into Gear

CINCINNATI, OCTOBER 20, 8:15 P.M.EDT

WITH THE 8:15 START to accommodate the West Coast audience, it was a chilly October night by the time Game 3 got underway. But Bowie Kuhn acted as if the game was taking place in August. He wore a brown sport coat, discarding the topcoat and hat he had worn earlier in the night before taking his place in the commissioner's box behind home plate. Cincinnati scribes immediately smirked, remembering the cold night in 1976 when Kuhn did the same. Many fans thought late October was simply too cold for baseball, but MLB had gradually pushed World Series games to that part of the month in order to maximize their playoff revenues. The commissioner did not want to acknowledge the obvious.

John McNamara mixed things up for Cincinnati ahead of Game 3. The Reds had been favored to win the Series before it started, but now they were in a deep hole. "I'm looking for a spark," said McNamara. Future Hall of Famer Johnny Bench, widely recognized as the greatest catcher of all time, would put on the "tools of ignorance" once again. Bench had not caught a game since April 29, a month before he fractured his left ankle sliding into second base. He told reporters he felt great despite playing in pain during most of the season's second half. The writers thought McNamara was either panicking or was just plain crazy, but the manager trusted that Bench could do it *one more time*. Bench had played first base in the first two games.

> Unlike the commissioner but much like Bill King, the Bay Area sportscaster, Reds' radio personality Marty Brennaman was adored by Reds fans for his impassioned play-by-play calls. The 31-year-old Brennaman replaced Al Michaels in 1974. His first broadcast for the Reds was April 4, 1974. Was he nervous? Not only was it his introduction to Reds Country, but history was staring him in the face. Atlanta's Hank Aaron was chasing Babe Ruth's all-time home run record, and he stood just one round-tripper away from tying The Great Bambino, the most famous player in baseball history. The world was listening. Brennaman greeted the fans and, just three batters in, made a flawless call of Aaron's record-tying home run.
>
> His broadcast partner was Joe Nuxhall, "the Ol' Left-hander." Unlike Brennaman, Nuxhall had played the game. He pitched primarily for the Reds during his career, retiring after the 1966 season, and immediately joined the radio booth. Outside of Cincinnati, Nuxhall was most known for being the youngest player ever to appear in a big-league game, having debuted for the Reds at the ripe old age of 15 on June 10, 1944. (He pitched just two-thirds of an inning and then waited eight years to return to the big leagues.) As color analyst, Nuxhall's down-home style endeared him to listeners.
>
> Brennaman and Nuxhall were different from each other in several ways. Brennaman was 13 years younger

than Nuxhall and liked to dress stylishly, while Nuxhall gave little thought to his appearance. With respect to broadcasting style, Brennaman was smooth and polished, while Nuxhall rambled when making calls. Nonetheless, they immediately gelled and became lifelong friends. They became so well known as a pair that fans would mail letters addressed to "Marty and Joe, Cincinnati, Ohio," and the US Postal Service would deliver the correspondence to Riverfront Stadium.

Brennaman and Nuxhall became fixtures in Reds Country. Broadcasting for a legendary team, it was not surprising that Brennaman was a "homer" on the air. He referred to the Reds as "we." As the team faded a bit in the late 1970s, Brennaman dropped the "we," became more neutral, and began to criticize the team more often. This change irked Reds ownership. When general manager Dick Wagner added a third broadcaster in 1980 to the booth because he thought Brennaman was too critical of the team, *The Cincinnati Enquirer* commissioned a poll to assess the popularity of Marty and Joe. Ownership backed off when 99 percent of respondents had no problem with the pair's newfound objectivity.

Reds' announcer Marty Brennaman was concerned before Game 3. As the game started, he gave his usual introduction: "If you're ready now, Rickey Henderson steps into the box. It's a balmy 48 degrees here in Cincinnati. Just like we like it." After Henderson singled to start the game, Brennaman worried out loud. "Boy, oh boy, oh boy. McNamara is rolling the dice tonight and he better hope Bench really is healthy. It will be front-page news if the A's are not trying to steal bases tonight."

Before Brennaman could finish, Henderson took off for second base on the first pitch to Murphy. "The pitch. Rickey's off, Bench throws a seed to Concepción. And he's out! How about that! McNamara may be elected mayor if Bench can slow the A's down." A back-and-forth affair ensued, the A's relying on power rather than speed while the Reds' veterans applied "their individual and collective talents" (per Brennaman) to stay within reach. Foster, Concepción, and Griffey each had two-out RBI singles. For good measure and the delight of the capacity crowd, Bench nailed Murphy attempting to swipe third base in the sixth.

Nonetheless, the Reds trailed the A's 4-3 in the bottom of the ninth when Foster led off with a frozen rope single to Henderson in left. Bench flew out to center, and Joe Nolan bunted Foster to second, raising Reds fans' hopes for a tying run while also raising Brennaman's blood pressure. "I'll tell ya what. This team hasn't bunted all year with no outs, and now they think it's wise to do it with one out? I can't imagine what McNamara was thinking. Knight's a solid hitter, but he's not Ty Cobb." Now, all that stood between the Reds and a 3-0 deficit was Ray Knight.

Pete Rose had been in a moment like this before. So had Tony Perez. And Joe Morgan. But by 1981, they were wearing other uniforms. Knight strode to the plate to a thunderous ovation, looked over his shoulder and winked at his girlfriend, LPGA star Nancy Lopez. She was seated in the third row behind the Reds' on-deck circle.

Knight was patient. Beard fell behind 3-1, the last pitch nearly sailing over the head of his battery mate, McKay. The crowd was delirious. Brennaman was on the call: "The 3-1 pitch. Knight windmills the bat. Swung on, it's a rocket into deep left field. Henderson is back, and that ball is gone! Home run!"

Nuxhall screamed, "Unbelievable!" in the background.

Brennaman continued: "Ray Knight has just raised the Reds from the dead with a clout over the 375 marker in left. The Reds are piling out of the dugout. Knight touches them all as the crowd is on its feet en masse here at Riverfront Stadium."

Then, he added his patented catch phrase: "And this one belongs to the Reds!" Brennaman continued, "A thrilling 5-4 comeback and they are dancing in the streets of Cincinnati. Knight single-handedly breathed new life into this Series, the Reds, and this city. Unbelievable!"

BOX SCORE

OAK   100 100 200   4 8 1

CIN   101 001 002   5 14 1

WP: Hume (1-0), LP: Beard (0-1)

Home Runs: Ray Knight (1)

In the ABC booth, Michaels had a flashback to 1972. In the deciding Game 5 of the NLCS, the Reds scored two in the bottom of the ninth, and Michaels was the Reds play-by-play man. "1 and 2. The windup and the pitch to Bench. It's hit into the air to deep right field. Back goes Clemente, at the fence. She's gone!" That home run tied the game, and the Reds later won the pennant on a wild pitch. But to Michaels, the Knight home run was eerily similar. He told the national audience: "I think the A's are in trouble."

All of a sudden, the Series was on again.

Beers, Bernie Stowe, and the best backstop of all time.

27

Bench's Banner Night

CINCINNATI, OCTOBER 21, 8:15 P.M. EDT

THE FIVE FRIENDS WHO ATTENDED THE TRIAL were able to secure tickets to Game 4 from Bernie Stowe, the Reds clubhouse manager. Bill O'Conner knew Stowe from the west side of Cincinnati, and he did not hesitate to ask for tickets. Stowe left them at will call, so after entering the stadium, the friends darted to their first-row seats in the third deck. They were 10 minutes late and missed Seaver escaping a bases-loaded jam in the top of the first.

Kneflin and Murphy unfurled the banner they had made and brought with them. When Finley and O'Conner returned with beers for the group, the bedsheet was already attached to the railing. It read 'THANKS JUDGE JACKSON' in large, red letters. A smattering of applause came from the crowd as the sign was displayed.

Seaver and McCatty were facing each other again. After two scoreless innings, six uniformed officers arrived at O'Conner's seats. "Boys, that's gotta come down. Orders from the boss," referring to Dick Wagner. The Reds never liked banners to be hung unless the Reds were the ones to hang them. While Oakland's Coliseum resembled a circus, Riverfront

Stadium was more like the inside of a Catholic grade school. There were no cheerleaders, no band, and most of all, no fan-made banners! The only music came from the organist in the stands behind home plate.

O'Conner yelled to Sharbell, "Joe get that thing down. We don't need to piss off Bernie Stowe!" Sharbell complied and placed the banner in the outstretched hands of one of the officers.

Across the field, in the Reds dugout, Stowe could see the banner come down. Unbeknownst to O'Conner, he was pleased. "Glad Bill and his posse are having fun." Stowe had no love for Wagner, particularly after he did the unthinkable after 1978 and let Pete Rose, a fellow West Sider, leave for the Phillies. Stowe would make sure security gave him the banner so he could return it to its rightful owners.

In the fourth, the Reds finally got to McCatty. After two were retired, Bench came to the plate. He had heard his mother yell to him from the stands a moment earlier, "Johnny, hit a home run!" Bench thought, "Sure, but against McCatty?" After working the count to full, the radio team made the call:

Marty: "Here's the pitch, Bench swings..."

Joe (in the background but easily heard): "Get outta here, get outta here!"

Marty: "... hits it deep to right field..."

Joe: "Get outta here!"

Marty: "Gone! That's an upper-tank job!"

Joe: "Byah! Byah!"

Listeners enjoyed it when Brennaman and Nuxhall commented on the same play. Bench's blast foreshadowed McCatty's early exit. The Reds scored three more in the frame thanks to a bases-clearing double by Collins, and they cruised to an easy 7-2 win. Bench, playing first base, went four for five with two RBI, and Nolan resumed his duties behind the plate. The A's did not attempt a steal once they were behind.

BOX SCORE

OAK   000 001 100   2 5 0

CIN   000 411 10X   7 15 0

WP: Seaver (1-1), LP: McCatty (1-1)

Home Runs: Johnny Bench (1), George Foster (1), Dave Concepción (1)

Would nostalgia provide an edge in the Series' swing game?

FICTION

28
Game 5 Reunion

CINCINNATI, OCTOBER 22, 8:15 P.M. EDT

THE REDS WERE HOT after a come-from-behind, dramatic win in Game 3, and an easy 7-2 victory in Game 4. Historical stats back up the importance of Game 5 in any World Series, with winners taking the Series about 66 percent of the time. Securing a victory was particularly pivotal for the Reds, as they would be returning to Oakland for Games 6 and 7. The memory of dropping two games there, albeit by just three combined runs, was painfully fresh in their minds. Cincinnati hoped their momentum from Games 3 and 4 would carry over to Game 5, which featured a rematch between Mario Soto and Rick Langford.

Reds owners and insurance magnates William and James Williams, along with minority owner Marge Schott, took a chance and saved the best pregame first pitch for Game 5. In fact, after Marian Spelman—a revered Cincinnati actress and singer—sang the national anthem, public address announcer Paul Sommerkamp came to the microphone. He informed the national audience that there would be two first pitches. At that, Pete Rose and Joe Morgan sprinted to the mound, while Tony Perez and Cesar Geronimo scampered to home plate!

The overflowing crowd went wild as Rose and Morgan delivered simultaneous tosses toward their former Machine mates. Bench, Concepción, Foster, and Griffey bounded over the dugout railing, and dugout photographers took one last picture of the "Great Eight" together at Riverfront Stadium.

Following Seaver, Soto was the second-best pitcher on the Reds staff in 1981. Seaver won Game 4 on three days' rest after only pitching on four or five days' rest during the regular season. Soto, on the other hand, pitched well in September and October on the two instances he took the mound on short rest—both complete games in which he allowed just one earned run.

Langford pitched four times on short rest in 1981, and he lost three of them. His last such outing was not effective. He allowed eight earned runs in seven innings en route to the A's 8-5 loss to the Chicago White Sox. Martin was somewhat concerned about using Langford after he had pitched in Oakland four days prior, but he thought the long delay between the regular season and the Series had allowed Langford sufficient time to rest before that. Nonetheless, the A's skipper instructed Matt Keough, his fourth starter, to be ready for a long relief appearance, if necessary.

Martin's planning was not necessary, as Langford kept the home crowd at bay, scattering just three hits through the first five innings. He did benefit from one of the oldest defensive tricks in baseball, one that, as Brennaman would say, "hasn't worked since Abner Doubleday invented the game." In the third inning, Oester was caught napping after a double. Oester took a few steps off second base as Langford played with the rosin bag to the side of the mound. Unbeknownst to Oester, the pitcher did not have the ball—shortstop Fred Stanley did, and he walked over and touched Oester for an out! To everyone's surprise, the hidden ball trick, used successfully just once before in the season, had worked in a

World Series game! Statisticians scrambled to determine whether such a ruse had ever happened in the Fall Classic. As far as anyone could determine, this was a first. Oester hung his head as he shuffled off the field, mortified by his inattention.

After Oakland catcher Mike Heath was stranded in the top half of the fourth, controversy ensued. Dave Collins walked to lead off the home half. The score was still 0-0. Bill King was on the call:

> Langford winds, kicks, and Griffey squares to bunt. Collins takes off. Griffey misses the pitch, and Heath throws to second off-balance. Griffey got in Heath's way! It is ruled a steal! Collins is safely on second, 180 feet from a go-ahead run for the Reds. This is zany, unbelievable, and folks, just plain wrong! Martin is on the field. He wants to know if the home plate umpire Rich Garcia saw what he saw: batter interference! Garcia listens, Billy bumps him, and Garcia throws Martin out of the game! The crowd is going bananas. Heath is in disbelief. Martin stomps to the dugout. This is a critical call, and Garcia is ignoring Billy's pleas.

This was not the first time Martin had been tossed from a World Series game. Ironically, his previous ejection was in the ninth inning of the final game (Game 4) of the 1976 Series against the Reds. In that game, Martin was tossed for throwing a ball from the dugout onto the field. But this was different; with the Series tied at two, there was a lot more baseball to be played.

After the situation calmed down, Langford kept his composure and coaxed a fly out by Griffey, induced Concepción to hit into a fielder's choice at third, and retired Foster on a soft fly to center. The score was still knotted at 0-0.

Soto was equally effective until the sixth, when Wayne Gross hit a laser over Foster's head. The carom off the left field fall wall eluded Foster, allowing Dwyane Murphy and Armas to score. Although Soto wriggled out of further trouble, the A's led 2-0.

After the Reds threatened in the sixth with a leadoff double by Collins, the Reds' bats were silent for the next six batters. Langford was cruising with a shutout through seven. Marty Brennaman announced the attendance to the radio audience to start the eighth: "56,407 turn out for tonight's titanic struggle . . . five six four zero seven." In the early years of his Reds' career, Brennaman had adopted "titanic struggle" as his traditional way of announcing the attendance figure at Reds' games, whether home or away. The crowd for this game set a Riverfront record, eclipsing the previous mark set in Game 5 of the 1975 Series by 14 ticket holders.

Reds' closer Tom Hume was summoned to pitch in the eighth, an unusual move by McNamara, but the skipper thought it gave the Reds the best shot of winning Game 5. Hume was effective, striking out Armas and Gross and sending the game to the bottom of the eighth. Art Fowler, who took over the strategy decisions after Martin was ejected, made a fateful move. He summoned Bob Owchinko to relieve Langford.

After Oester doubled over Henderson's head, pinch hitter Driessen awakened the standing room–only crowd with a screamer that ricocheted off of Gross's glove at third, the first time the fielder had not snared a seemingly sure base hit in the Series. Oester advanced to third. After pinch runner Rafael Landestoy replaced Driessen, the pressure turned on Collins.

In the second half of the regular season, Collins sputtered. And sputtered. And sputtered some more. Collins hit .214 with a .307 on-base percentage. In the first half, Collins's on-base plus slugging percentage (OPS) was .829. In the second half, it was .597. So in essence, Collins went from hitting like Hall of Famer Don Mattingly (.830 career OPS) in the first 54 games he played in 1981, to hitting like journeyman infielder Mario Guerrero (.597 career OPS) in the last 41.

Now, Collins faced Owchinko with the Reds in a position to tie Game 5. Owchinko, who would appear in 49 games for the Reds in 1984, fell behind 2-0. Not wanting to walk Collins and load the bases with the Machine veterans coming up, the lefty's next pitch caught too much of the plate, and Collins was equal to the occasion. He scorched a smash off the elbow of shortstop Stanley. Landestoy was running on the pitch. Brennaman called the tying run. "A one-hop tracer off Stanley and into short left field! Oester scores! And that baby is going to get the speedy Landestoy in all the way from first base, and I mean he was picking 'em up and layin 'em down. We're tied!"

Fowler visited the mound to check in with Owchinko. He had the lefty-lefty matchup he wanted with Griffey coming to the plate, but then again Griffey was one of the four Machine veterans. Owchinko was getting pummeled, and Griffey had hit .311 during the regular season. Nonetheless, Fowler decided to let Owchinko face one more batter. Brennaman called the action: "High drive, right field, that baby is hit a ton, and it's a 4-2 ballgame! That is your primary definition of a hanging curveball, and Griffey just showed Mr. Owchinko why you should not do that! Collins scores, and Griffey touches 'em all."

Hume finished off the deflated A's in the ninth, and the critical Game 5 belonged to the Reds.

BOX SCORE

OAK	000 002 000	2	9 0
CIN	000 000 04X	4	10 1

WP: Hume (2-0), **LP:** Owchinko (0-1)

Home Runs: Ken Griffey (1)

As the A's quickly retreated to the locker room, a raucous Cincinnati crowd remained and cheered their heroes. Three blocks north, there was a party brewing on Fountain Square as if the Series were over. The players knew there was still plenty of work to do as both teams headed to Oakland. The teams were relieved that there was a travel day before Game 6.

Mario Soto

Mother Nature

makes an appearance.

FICTION

29

Rain, Rain, Go Away

OAKLAND, OCTOBER 24-25

GAME 6 WAS SCHEDULED FOR SATURDAY, October 24, but heavy rains were in the forecast. During the regular season, the home team always enjoyed the authority to postpone or delay a game. In the Series, though, that power was in the commissioner's hands.

Forecasters from the National Weather Service, traveling from Fremont, California, at MLB's request, greeted Kuhn as he arrived at noon. "Commissioner, it does not look good. A low-pressure system from the Pacific will bring thunderstorms, heavy rain, and potential flooding through the night. The weather may not clear until Monday, two days from now." Kuhn frowned. He was hoping the forecast would be better.

Kuhn huffed to the A's offices, looking for owner Marvin Davis, but Davis found him first, saying "I've talked to the Reds. We're calling the game, Mr. Kuhn." Before Davis could continue, Kuhn reminded him that was *his* decision. "Let me talk to my people."

Kuhn feared the worst. He knew the historical criticisms of October baseball. Professional baseball had battled rain issues during the Series since the early 1900s. The worst was a six-day delay between Games 3 and 4 in 1911, ironically a series between the New York Giants and the Philadelphia A's, the team that migrated to Oakland 56 years later. In 1925, Game 7 was delayed one day, then played the next day in rain and fog. In 1962, the Yankees and Giants played just one game over a seven-day span, as both Games 5 and 6 were pushed back by rain. Most recently, Game 6 between the Reds and Red Sox was delayed three days in 1975.

Kuhn optimistically recalled that the 1975 Series won by the Big Red Machine was considered the greatest World Series ever played, and the delayed Game 6 was considered the greatest World Series game. He was there when Carlton Fisk waved a 10th-inning, game-winning home run into fair territory. He also knew the 1975 Series averaged 35 million viewers, the largest ever, and Games 6 and 7 were by far the most-watched games of all time—41 and 51 million, respectively.

Neither team showed up that afternoon for batting or fielding practice. Finally, around 4:00, Kuhn announced the postponement until the next evening. The media quickly pounced on him for the long wait.

On Sunday, the commissioner directed both teams to prepare to play. Reds skipper McNamara called Kuhn "nuts," and Martin threatened to tell his players to stay home, but he eventually cooled down. The field was nearly unplayable, so neither manager wanted to risk injury to his players. Nonetheless, the commissioner dug in his heels about waiting out the rain, which meant ticket holders had to brave the elements or risk missing out. ABC came on the air in the remote chance that the game would get underway. Al Michaels opined, "Ladies and gentlemen, the rain is subsiding and Commissioner Kuhn says they'll wait it out. Does he know something the weather folks do not?"

Given the three-hour difference in time zones, Cincinnatians and East Coast fans worried that they might have to miss the deciding game if the delay went on too long. Michaels' remarks came at 8:15 Eastern time, and

Kuhn waited two more hours before conceding. The critics were furious again, this time blaming Kuhn for waiting so long when the delay seemed inevitable. Kuhn wisely declined interviews. Cincinnati Channel 9 TV reporter John Popovich jokingly referred to the "Split World Series" and wondered on air whether Judge Jackson might need to compel a move to a fairer weather locale, such as Los Angeles.

A's summon a 1972 Series hero for good luck.

30

Reds' History Repeats

<u>OAKLAND, OCTOBER 26, 5:15 P.M. PST</u>

O N MONDAY, THE SKY FINALLY CLEARED and the grounds crew worked most of the day to sweep the water off the warning tracks and prepare the dirt infield, pitcher's mound, and batting circle. Game on!

In the 1972 World Series, Oakland led 3-2 after five games and needed to win one of two games on the road to secure their first of three consecutive world championships. (The A's franchise had previously won five titles when it was based in Philadelphia). Now, the Reds were leading 3-2, and they could wrap up the Series with one win on the road. Would Cincinnati, on the cusp of a third championship in seven years, equal what Oakland accomplished from 1972 to 1974?

As much as they enjoyed playing in front of their fans at Riverfront Stadium, the Reds did not want to chance a Game 7. They wanted to seize the day and end the Series in six games. McNamara penciled in Seaver to start Game 6, this time on the more typical four days' rest, thanks to two days of rain. Martin turned to McCatty for his third start of the Series.

The pregame festivities featured Gene Tenace, an almost-obscure backup catcher for the A's in 1972. Tenace hit just five home runs during the 1972 regular season, but he belted four home runs in the Series against the Reds while amassing a .913 slugging percentage. That output was enough to eclipse the long-standing Series record of .900 set by Babe Ruth. Reds fans were apoplectic over Tenace's sudden productivity, which peaked at the worst possible time. One fan, Elwood F. King, was even arrested with a loaded revolver and an open bottle of whiskey after saying, "Somebody ought to kill the SOB because he's killing the Reds." That threat and others necessitated FBI protection for Tenace during the remainder of the Series, prompting Tenace to remark, "It scares me, but I'll play." And play he did.

On this evening, there were no threats, just a deafening standing ovation for Tenace, who was introduced to the crowd after other fan favorites from the 1972 club: Vida Blue, Rollie Fingers, Joe Rudi, Dick Green, Bert Campaneris, and Reggie Jackson. (To the fans' dismay, a hamstring injury had kept Jackson out of the 1972 Series). Tenace and Blue then reversed their erstwhile roles, with Tenace throwing the ceremonial pitch to Blue, prompting another roar from the crowd.

The fans settled into their seats, but for the first six innings, things looked glum for the home side. Neither Seaver nor McCatty survived seven innings, though Seaver performed slightly better than McCatty despite being unusually wild. Two home runs by Bench coupled with RBI doubles by Foster and Concepción staked the Reds to a 5-1 lead through six, quieting the raucous crowd. The only excitement for Oakland fans came from a few waves led by Krazy George, but even those were not as exuberant as in Game 1. Nine outs stood between Cincinnati and a third world championship in seven years.

Beginning in the seventh, the A's clawed back against the Reds' succession of hurlers. After Seaver gave up a couple singles to start the frame, McNamara signaled to the bullpen with his right arm. Bruce Berenyi, who started Game 3 and likely would have been positioned to start Game 6 had it not been for the rain delay, came trotting in as A's fans began to sing "Billy Ball" to agitate the Reds. Berenyi had pitched only once in relief during the season. He got off to a strong start, striking out Drumright on three pitches.

Armas was next. Worried the A's would steal, Berenyi threw a fastball that Armas hammered to right field. The ball barely stayed in the park, scoring Henderson and Murphy. Gross then rocketed a 3-1 pitch from Berenyi into the gap in right, scoring Armas. Suddenly it was a 5-4 game. After this shelling, McNamara had seen enough, forgoing his stable of relievers and summoning starter Mike LaCoss instead.

LaCoss was a cool customer and had been in this type of situation before. In the 1979 All-Star Game at Seattle's Kingdome—during a time when All-Star games still meant something—LaCoss was called upon to keep the game close after the American League took a 6-5 lead. With the bases loaded in the last half of the sixth inning, LaCoss retired Don Baylor on a force play to end that frame. He went on to pitch a scoreless seventh. The National League later rallied to win with single runs in the eighth and ninth, extending the NL's consecutive All-Star Game winning streak to eight. Two years later, McNamara hoped LaCoss could relieve once again, but this time, he had to hold the lead that was already in place.

With Gross on second and one out, LaCoss reprised his All-Star Game performance and then some. With the crowd losing its collective mind after Gross's double, LaCoss struck out five consecutive batters, two in the seventh and three in the eighth.

The Reds, having gone scoreless since the sixth inning, were counting on their pitching staff to see them through. As the bottom of the ninth was about to begin, LaCoss pleaded with McNamara to let him finish the game. "Mac, we need to win tonight." But McNamara followed the same strategy he had employed most of the year. He turned to Hume, who had led the team in saves during the regular season and had saved Game 5. LaCoss was having a spectacular night, but after the pitcher's so-so regular season, McNamara took the safe route, playing it "by the book" to hold Cincinnati's one-run advantage.

After retiring the first two batters, Hume needed just one out to secure the Series, but he became noticeably rattled by the frenzy inside the Coliseum chanting "boom boom." Hume was sometimes ridiculed by the opposing team's fans with the nickname "Boom Boom Hume" for having given up long balls on occasion. His first pitch to Armas landed close to the top of the 30-foot high backstop behind the plate. On the next pitch, Armas doubled to center, connecting with a fastball grooved down the middle. Gross followed with an absolute moonshot that nearly exited the Coliseum on the next pitch. As Armas scored, Gross dove head first into second base. Tie game!

Bill King was stunned. Like most others, he assumed Hume would close the door. The champagne in the visitors' locker room was ready to be popped, and the locker room was covered with plastic wrap to protect the furniture. ABC's crew was already there for postgame interviews with the Big Red Machine-era stars: Bench, Foster, Concepción, and Griffey.

It had all happened so quickly. Two pitches, and Game 6 was tied. Said King, "Folks, I'm not sure how to describe what I just saw! One of the game's most reliable relievers just melted down before 47,891 witnesses. This crowd may never settle down, and McNamara has just yanked his closer. Here comes Bair. The A's seem intent to force a Game 7. What a comeback! This is crazy."

Doug Bair had not had a particularly good season, but he had stellar moments in the past. Bair had saved 28 games for Sparky Anderson in 1978, and now he was being called upon to stop the bleeding in a game that the Reds had all but won just 10 minutes earlier. Jim Spencer, who was eager to be a hero, lined a single down the left-field line. Gross ran through the stop sign at third hoping to score the winning run, but Foster, who had shaded Spencer toward the left-field stands, came up firing and threw a strike to Bench as Gross slid. "He's out," exclaimed home plate umpire Dick Stello. Everyone knew he was out, and no argument ensued. This late offensive flurry gave the A's new life, while the Reds were just relieved they had dodged a bullet.

Everything seemed to calm down in the 10th inning, with both teams going down in order. Reds' batters had no success in the 11th. McNamara knew Bair was tired and turned to Paul Moskau to face the top of the A's order.

Moskau had not pitched since the end of the regular season three weeks earlier. He had not fared well in that appearance, giving up five runs in two-thirds of an inning. Rickey Henderson strode to the plate. Moskau knew a walk would put the game's most prolific base stealer on first. Shaking off Bench, Moskau decided to challenge Henderson with a fastball. As clocks on the East Coast struck midnight, Rickey Henderson walloped a high, arcing fly ball down the left-field line. Henderson waved two arms, as if he could keep it from going foul. It curled ever so slightly before sailing around the fair pole. Home run!

Chants of "Rickey, Rickey" rang throughout the Coliseum, and his teammates mobbed him as he jumped on home plate.

BOX SCORE

CIN	012 002 000 00	5	9	0
OAK	001 000 301 01	6	10	0

WP: Dave Beard (1-0), **LP:** Paul Moskau (0-1)

Home Runs: Johnny Bench 2 (3), Rickey Henderson (1)

Another Game 7 was in the cards between the two storied franchises. The Reds meandered to the clubhouse, not believing they had just blown a four-run lead. Bench tore down the plastic covering the locker stalls, muttered an expletive, and ordered that the champagne be placed back in the coolers. He thought all the postgame preparations had jinxed his team.

Can the Reds avenge 1972 and join baseball immortality?

31

Here We Go Again!

OAKLAND, OCTOBER 27, 5:15 P.M. PST

THE CINCINNATI REDS WERE IN FAMILIAR TERRITORY. The franchise had survived the 1975 Series after losing Game 6 in Boston on a similar heartbreak. First Carlton Fisk, now Rickey Henderson. Only five Reds players from that team were still around. Gone were Rose, Perez, Morgan, and Geronimo. Still remaining, though, were four of the "Great Eight": Bench, Griffey, Foster, and Concepción, along with Driessen, a steady contributor for the Reds since 1973. McNamara would need to summon his inner Sparky Anderson after a difficult night's sleep.

McNamara called Bench in the morning. "Johnny, I don't plan to do anything differently tonight, but I'd like you to address the team and talk about 1975."

Bench replied, "Mac, happy to do that. I know we will be alright." Bench was respected by his teammates as one of baseball's all-time greats, but he had never called such a meeting. "What's up?" the players wondered when Bench brought them together before the game. His message was short and simple: "Boys, a few of us have played in a Game 7. Go out there, play your best, and enjoy the experience. I'll pop the champagne later!"

The assembled group responded with a resounding "Hell, yes!" and then went out to the field to warm up.

Since Game 3 starter Bruce Berenyi had been used in Game 6, McNamara turned to a different starter on short rest: Soto. Martin did the same and put Langford on the mound. Oddsmakers favored Oakland.

The A's got off to a fast start. Soto gave up three early runs on an RBI single by Armas in the first, and a two-run blast by Henderson—the MVP favorite after his Game 6 heroics—in the third. The Big Red Machine was in need of refueling. As for the fans in the Coliseum, they sensed blood.

After Griffey lined a single in the fourth and stole second easily, Bench came to the plate with two outs. Langford quickly fell behind 3-0, then 3-2, and Heath held out his right hand for an intentional walk. Bench acted relaxed as if he expected to walk, but when the next pitch sailed into the strike zone, Bench launched a 455-foot home run into the center-field bleachers. Bench anticipated the trickery, remembering that the A's pulled a similar stunt nine years earlier in the 1972 Series. Griffey gave a high five to Bench as he crossed home plate, making the score 3-2. Driessen kept the momentum going with a drive into the left-field seats two pitches later, tying it at 3-3. Fortunately for A's fans, the damage ended when Langford retired Knight. Neither team scored in the fifth inning.

Oakland came to bat in the sixth and after one out, Soto gave up singles to Keith Drumright and Armas. The A's had runners on the corners and were looking for a tie-breaking hit. Instead, Gross hit a high chopper up the first base line in front of the plate, and Bench pounced from behind the plate. He turned to tag Drumright, who was racing home, but National League plate umpire Dick Stello got in the way as he positioned himself to call the ball fair or foul. As Drumright slid to avoid the catcher, Bench tagged Drumright with his glove, but the ball was in his right hand! Fortunately for the Reds, Drumright missed the plate. Stello fell backward on the ground but still managed to call "out!" as if he had seen the play.

Martin vaulted from the dugout. "Dick, are you blind? Bench never tagged him! The ball was in his right hand!" As Martin and Stello went nose to nose, Martin motioned to the field umpires for help, but Stello held firm. Drumright, who assumed he tagged home, rushed in to argue, standing on home plate. Stello refused to ask his colleagues for help and the call stood.

The ABC broadcast crew reviewed the replay, after which Keith Jackson declared, "Three misses must make an out. Bench missed the tag, Drumright missed the plate, and Stello missed the call! What a Series we have!" Jackson then turned to Al Michaels, the former Reds announcer, and asked, "Does it matter that Drumright later stood on the plate?"

Michaels retorted, "We don't know, but the score remains tied!" Meanwhile, a chorus of boos echoed throughout the Coliseum from fans who could not see exactly what happened.

When the game resumed, Soto retired Spencer on a weak grounder to first to bring the inning to a close. The fans continued to spew venom on Stello, but the Reds breathed a sigh of relief. Concepción had seen Drumright stand on home plate during the squabble over Stello's call. He turned to McNamara as he ran to the dugout after the groundout and said, "We got a break. He was safe. Maybe this is our year!"

Reds' fans saw their hopes rise further when Griffey, Foster, and Bench promptly launched home runs in the seventh, one of them scoring Concepción after he doubled. The Reds enjoyed a comfortable lead at 7-3. Bench's bomb was his fifth in the last four games, tying Reggie "Mr. October" Jackson for the most ever in a single World Series. LaCoss and Bair held the lead, and the A's never managed another base runner until the ninth when they loaded the bases with two outs off Reds closer Hume.

When Cliff Johnson was announced as a pinch hitter for light-hitting Fred Stanley, another standing ovation occurred, as A's fans were thirsting for Johnson to hit in a critical spot. Johnson had had a great season, mostly as a designated hitter with an occasional spot start at first. He was second on the club with 17 home runs in the shortened season behind Armas, but the Reds had neutralized him thus far. Martin preferred to use left-handed Drumright against McNamara's steady array of right-handed pitching. Now, *if only* he could hit a grand slam. The fans also knew that Henderson, the hero from the night before, stood in the on-deck circle hoping for another magical moment.

All eyes turned to McNamara. Would he pull Hume? The answer came quickly. McNamara appeared to be a statue as he stayed on his perch in the dugout, trusting Hume to hold the lead. As a sellout crowd stomped and shook the Coliseum, Johnson fouled a change-up deep into the upper deck in right field before hitting a sinking liner to center. Griffey raced in and made a spectacular diving grab to seal the victory! It was Griffey's third great catch in the Series.

BOX SCORE

CIN 000 300 400 7 10 0

OAK 102 000 000 3 6 1

WP: Soto (1-0), LP: Langford (0-1), Sv: Hume (1)

Home Runs: Rickey Henderson (2), Johnny Bench 2 (5), Dan Driessen (1), George Foster (2), Ken Griffey (2)

The Reds won Game 7, 7-3, clinching the Machine's third championship in seven seasons. Henderson looked dismayed as the Reds romped on his home field. For his part, Martin broke six bats in the dugout.

Brennaman exclaimed from the booth, "And this World Series belongs to the Reds! Boy, oh boy! What a Series!" On the field, Bench jumped into the grasp of Hume as the players and coaches celebrated on the field. ABC's Keith Jackson and Commissioner Kuhn proceeded to the podium that had been set up at home plate and presented the World Series trophy to team owners William (Bill) and James Williams, with Bill's son and future owner Thomas Williams—age 23—at their side.

Jackson shouted "Whoa, Nelly!"—the trademark phrase he often voiced after an exciting play in college football—prompting Bill Williams to exclaim, "You aren't kidding. What a journey! Thank the Lord that justice was served and our Big Red Machine is still rolling!"

After Williams concluded his remarks, Kuhn made an unusual announcement: "I am happy to do something never before done after a World Series. We are declaring that four outstanding players—Johnny Bench, Ken Griffey, Dave Concepción, and George Foster—are this year's co-MVPs!" The four stars looked sheepishly at each other with wide grins, and then embraced for the last time on the field together as Cincinnati Reds. Foster screamed "Hurrah!" into the microphone. Even the Oakland fans who were still hanging around came to their feet with a standing ovation for the collective accomplishments of the Reds' mighty foursome.

The Oakland media was echoing the concerns voiced by Martin. "Bench never tagged Drumright! How could Stello not see that, or even check with the crew? That changed the whole ballgame. We were robbed." That evening's sports page led off with the headline, "Three misses make an out," commenting on Bench missing the tag, Drumright missing the plate (but later standing on it), and Stello missing the call.

Back in Cincinnati, the students who attended the trial—O'Conner, Finley, Kneflin, Murphy, and Sharbell—sped once again from one of their favorite taverns, the Crow's Nest, to Cincinnati's main gathering space,

Fountain Square. The square was lit up in red, and the four figures with animals seemed to lap up the flowing water from the Tyler Davidson fountain. An estimated 15,000 fans reveled in James Brown's classic hit, "I Feel Good," blaring from nearby speakers. Cincinnati's King Records owned Federal Records, which launched Brown's career, so the song had a connection to Cincinnati that only some of the partiers realized. Nonetheless, everyone was indeed feeling good!

Far, Smack, and Queen couldn't help but feel vindicated. They watched the entire Series at Mehlman's Pub while navigating their third year of law school. On this night, Mehlman's was the hottest bar in Columbus, with a long line of patrons patiently waiting to enter. An exception was granted to George Wright, who arrived late to congratulate his clients. "Mission accomplished!" he exclaimed as he hugged the jubilant law students.

Kuhn observed the overnight ratings the next morning. Despite his contorted efforts to rekindle interest in baseball after the strike, the ensuing Series accomplished his original goal and lined the owners' pockets. A record 50 million viewers tuned into Game 7, and the audience share was a whopping 59 percent—another record. Not even the National Football League could match those numbers. Kuhn's bosses got what they wanted, and the players could rest assured that free agency was here to stay.

EPILOGUE
What *Really* Happened

As previously noted, up until our make-believe World Series, the even-numbered chapters of this book (through chapter 22) accurately recount the twists and turns of MLB's bifurcated 1981 season. The odd-numbered chapters offer a fictionalized account of what might have been had the legal wrangling of three die-hard baseball fans been successful. The paragraphs below chronicle what *really happened* after Bowie Kuhn announced his convoluted split-season approach to the playoffs.

The lawsuit. A lawsuit was filed by three Ohio State University law students after the split season concluded, but their future employers and a federal judge urged them in no uncertain terms to file a voluntary dismissal. They reluctantly complied and ensconced themselves at Mehlman's Pub in Columbus to drown their sorrows.

The postseason. The playoffs went on as planned. The A's swept the Royals in the AL Division Series, and the Yankees edged Milwaukee 3-2. The Yankees went on to trounce the A's in the ALCS. The Dodgers and Expos each prevailed 3-2 in their NLDS series over the Astros and the

Phillies, respectively. The Dodgers edged Montreal 3-2 in the NLCS, with Rick Monday's go-ahead home run in the top of the ninth making the difference in Game 5.

After the Yankees won the first two games of the World Series, Los Angeles rallied from an 0-2 deficit, winning Games 3, 4, and 5 by one run apiece. Game 6 at Yankee Stadium was postponed by one day due to rain. When play resumed, the Dodgers romped to a 9-2 win to claim their first world championship since 1965. Three Dodger position players, Pedro Guerrero, Ron Cey, and Steve Yeager, were named co-MVPs.

Two more members of the Great Eight depart. On November 4, 1981, Ken Griffey, a nine-year Reds veteran, was traded for pitcher Brian Ryder, the Yankees' first-round pick in 1978, as well as a player to be named later (pitcher Freddie Toliver). Ryder never made the majors, and Toliver barely pitched for the Reds, logging just 10 innings in 1984.

George Foster lasted a little over two months longer than Griffey. After 11 seasons in Cincinnati, Foster was moved to the Mets on February 10, 1982, in exchange for catcher/infielder Alex Trevino and pitchers Greg Harris and Jim Kern. Only Kern provided anything of value for the Reds, recording an ERA of 2.84 in 76 innings in 1982.

Other 1981 regulars leave town. Though not members of the Big Red Machine, two other regulars from the 1981 Reds departed. Dave Collins signed with the Yankees as a free agent, while Ray Knight was shipped to Houston for outfielder Cesar Cedeno, who at age 30 was way past his prime. Knight made the 1982 All-Star team as an Astro.

The nadir of 1982. If 1981 was a dream return to contention for the Reds, 1982 was a nightmare from beginning to end. Cincinnati finished 61-101, dropping 100 games for the first time in franchise history. The 1982

Reds' winning percentage (37.7%) remains tied for fourth-worst in the history of the team.

Johnny Bench (1983) and Dave Concepción (1988) retire.

The final two members of the Great Eight to leave the Reds were Johnny Bench and Dave Concepción. As it turns out, Bench was serious about hanging up his face mask and shin guards. In 1981, he played seven games at catcher and 38 at first base. From 1982-83, Bench caught just six games, spending most of his time at third base with occasional spells at first. He made the All-Star team for the 14th and final time in 1983. In his final at-bat on September 29, 1983, he hit a pinch-hit, two-run single at Riverfront Stadium. The Reds retired Bench's No. 5 in 1986, and in 1989 the greatest catcher to ever play the game was inducted into the National Baseball Hall of Fame, accumulating 96 percent of the vote in his first year of eligibility.

Concepción made the last of his eight All-Star teams in 1982, winning MVP honors after hitting a home run off Dennis Eckersley. Concepción remained the Reds' primary shortstop through the 1985 season when he was 37. He retired at the end of the 1988 season. By then future Hall of Famer Barry Larkin had made his first All-Star team in his second season as the Reds' everyday shortstop. The Reds' retired Concepción's No. 13 in 2007.

Reds, A's meet in 1990 World Series.

The Reds and A's did meet again in the World Series, but not until 1990. The underdog Reds avenged their 1972 Series loss, sweeping the A's. With that win, the franchise achieved a nine-game World Series winning streak (Game 7 in 1975 and two four-game sweeps in 1976 and 1990).

Fictional World Series Simulation

While our imagined Series between the Reds and the A's is purely fictional, we aimed to describe the on-field action in a way that was believable based on both teams' 1981 performance. Thankfully, we did not need to rely only on our own analysis of team and player stats to do that.

To boost our plausibility, we simulated the fictional Series many times on Whatifsports.com, an all-sports simulation website. In our simulations, Oakland was always the home team in Games 1 and 2, and in 6 and 7 if the Series went that long. Cincinnati was the home team in Games 3, 4, and 5 (if necessary). Reds' fans who still bear a grudge about MLB's fabricated playoff structure in 1981 will be delighted (or aggrieved?) to know the Reds won a majority of the simulated Series.

An All-Sports Simulation Website, *www.whatifsports.com*

Bibliography

Writing this book would not have been possible without the aid of the following books, magazines, newspapers, published works, and websites.

Books

Golenbock, Peter.
Wild, High and Tight: The Life and Death of Billy Martin, 1994.

Helyar, John.
The Lords of The Realm: The Real History of Baseball, 1995.

Katz, Jeff.
Split Season: 1981, 2015.

Korr, Charles P.
The End of Baseball As We Knew It: The Players Union, 1960-81, 2002.

Shales, Tom.
Those Guys Have All the Fun: Inside the World of ESPN, 2011.

Newspapers, News Sources, and Periodicals

Cincinnati Magazine	*Los Angeles Times*
San Francisco Chronicle	*Sports Illustrated*
St. Louis Post-Dispatch	*The Associated Press*
The Athletic	*The Cincinnati Enquirer*
The Cincinnati Post	*The Washington Post*
The New York Times	*United Press*
United Press International	

Websites

Answers.com	Baseball-almanac.com
Baseball-reference.com	CNN.com
Fangraphs.com	MLB.com
MLBPA.com	Newspapers.com
Nmathletics.com	Reds.com
Retrosheet.com	Whatifsports.com
Wikipedia.com	

Other Sources

Kennesaw State University Department of Economics, Finance and Quantitative Analysis

National Baseball Hall of Fame

Society for American Baseball Research

Photo Credits

Photos of Reds players and manager courtesy of Rhodes/Klumpe Reds Hall of Fame Collection.

The use of the Reds logo and the phrase "Big Red Machine" on the front cover is courtesy of a license from Major League Baseball.

Back cover photo courtesy of the Cincinnati Reds.

About the Authors

RANDY FREKING is a lifelong baseball fan and current cohost of the podcast, WE LOVE OUR TEAM. He lives in Cincinnati with his wife, Sue, and they have four adult children and enough grandchildren to field a starting lineup. They are blessed with many nieces and nephews, including coauthor Grant.

A retired lawyer versed in labor law, Randy is the author of *Cincinnati's 150-Year Opening Day History: The Hoopla Started With A Parade* (Cincinnati Book Publishing, 2018); coauthor with Mike Zilliox of *@Titanicstruggle: The Best of Marty Brennaman* (Cincinnati Book Publishing, 2020); author of *The Real Employee Handbook* (CreateSpace Independent Publishing Platform, 2012); and author of the *ABA Consumer Guide to Employee Rights* (American Bar Association, 2015). Randy was listed in every edition of *Best Lawyers in America* from 1994 through his retirement in 2020.

Randy graduated from The Ohio State University College of Law, along with classmates and avid baseball fans, Jim Neary and Bob Kiss. Neary and Kiss, bearing the pseudonyms of Jim Far and Bob Smack in the fictional chapters herein, were Randy's co-conspirators in filing the lawsuit that inspired this book.

GRANT FREKING is also a lifelong baseball fan and overall sports enthusiast. He lives in Cincinnati, surrounded by family and friends.

A journalist/writer since age 16 and a graduate of The Ohio State University, Grant currently works in marketing and communications for the University of Cincinnati. He has written for a host of brands, magazines, newspapers, and websites, covering everything from high school gymnastics meets in Lafayette, Indiana, to signage and graphics conventions in Las Vegas. His writing has garnered honors from the Public Relations Society of America's Cincinnati chapter, the Society of Professional Journalists, Indiana Associated Press Media Editors, Hoosier State Press Association, and Indiana High School Baseball Coaches Association.

He is eternally grateful for Randy's support, wisdom, and presence in his life.

"A rollicking treatise from Uncle Randy and nephew Grant. They elevate the true story of the highway robbery of the 1981 Cincinnati Reds, who had the best overall record in MLB that year, into a whopper of a yarn with a satisfying and serendipitous ending. Mesmerizing from the first page to the last. Baseball as it should be!"

JOHN ERARDI
Award-winning Cincinnati sportswriter and author of multiple books on the Cincinnati Reds

Courtesy of the Cincinnati Reds

"This book proves the cliché that truth is stranger than fiction. Here, the fiction makes more sense than the historical facts!"

JACK GREINER
Noted First Amendment attorney, writer and cohost of the podcast, "WE LOVE OUR TEAM"